The Politburo

About the Book and Author

Using both qualitative and quantitative analysis, Dr. Laird has compiled a unique catalog of data on every member of the Politburo since 1917. Central to the analysis is a "change index" that provides a running measure of politically motivated changes in Politburo membership. Examining continuities and changes in the Politburo over the years, the author shows that within each of the major leadership eras there were important subperiods marking significant policy changes. He also uses the index, along with other empirical measures, to explain successes and failures of specific policy initiatives. In the final chapters, Dr. Laird identifies the major constraints facing the post-Brezhnev leadership and offers evidence that Gorbachev will likely attempt major economic and administrative reforms, especially in the critical area of agriculture. Because Gorbachev does not yet have the "votes" to initiate reforms, however, major efforts cannot be expected until later in the 1980s when a second period of "the Gorbachev era" is expected to begin.

Dr. Roy D. Laird is professor of political science and Soviet and East European studies at the University of Kansas.

We the leaders are responsible for everything. Therefore, we must understand everything, recognizing right from wrong and good from evil, supporting the right way and vanquishing the wrong way.

—Khrushchev, in a speech
to agricultural workers in 1957

Somebody said that foreign policy is a continuation of domestic policy. If that is so, then I ask you to ponder one thing. If we in the Soviet Union are setting ourselves such truly grandiose plans in the domestic sphere, then what are the external conditions that we need to be able to fulfill those domestic plans?

—Gorbachev, in his September 9, 1985,
Time interview

The Politburo

Demographic Trends, Gorbachev, and the Future

Roy D. Laird

Westview Press / Boulder and London

Westview Special Studies on the Soviet Union and Eastern Europe

---

This Westview softcover edition was manufactured on our own premises using equipment and methods that allow us to keep even specialized books in stock. It is printed on acid-free paper and bound in softcovers that carry the highest rating of the National Association of State Textbook Administrators, in consultation with the Association of American Publishers and the Book Manufacturers' Institute.

Published in 1986 in the United States of America by Westview Press, Inc.; Frederick A. Praeger, Publisher; 5500 Central Avenue, Boulder, Colorado 80301

Library of Congress Catalog Card Number: 86-050121
ISBN: 0-8133-7198-8

Composition for this book was provided by the author.
This book was produced without formal editing by the publisher.

Printed and bound in the United States of America

The paper used in this publication meets the requirements of the American National Standard for Permanence of Paper for Printed Library Materials Z39.48-1984.

6 5 4 3 2 1

To Betty, Claude, David, Diana, Heather,
and John, "intellectuals" all!

Contents

Tables, Figures, and Profiles

TABLES

FIGURES

PROFILES

Preface

This book is intended to add a new dimension to the understanding of the Politburo of the Central Committee of the Communist Party of the Soviet Union.

I have systematically organized and analyzed available biographical information on the 83 individuals (82 men and one woman) who have served as full voting members of the Politburo from 1917 until mid-November, 1985. Catalogued in the chronological listing of the incumbents (six individuals were removed only to be returned at a later date for a second term as full voting members) according to the date of their entry into the Politburo as full voting members (offered in the Appendix), and in the Politburo profiles for each of the historical periods I have identified, the reader will find such data as dates of birth, nationality, parents' occupation, education, date of entry into the Party, dates of entry and exit from the Politburo, etc. My belief is that when such data are systematically analyzed, including the identification of changes and trends over time, new insights into the nature of Politburo politics arise.

In sum, this study is a systematic empirical analysis of the demographic changes in the membership of the Politburo which, when seen in light of historical knowledge, hopefully, will enhance our understanding of Soviet leadership politics.

Roy D. Laird

Acknowledgments

As discussed below, I am enormously indebted to the Munich-based researchers in the former Institute for the Study of the USSR, and those now at RFE/RL, for producing the Soviet biographies that served as my data base. Also, I must thank Professors Ronald Francisco and Alec Nove for their reading of the work while in preparation and their most helpful suggestions, which have added significantly to the work. Further, I must thank April Cash for typing the Profiles and both Wes Hubert and Ken Jordan whose wizardry with the computer was indispensable. Most of all, I must thank Betty Laird for her assistance which, as always, went far, far beyond catching my split infinitives. As in all of our work, the Lairds are a writing team. Finally, The University of Kansas is a superb base for conducting such research. Of course, all of the faults are my responsibility.

R.D.L.

PART ONE

An Empirical Study of the Politburo

This part of the study lays the base for what follows.

In the first chapter, "The Data Base," I discuss in detail the source of the data used in the empirical analysis, the methodology and approach employed and some of the major problems and shortcomings involved.

In chapter 2, "The Qualitative Politburo Environment," I lay out my understanding of the history and nature of the Soviet political system, particularly in its application to Politburo of the analyst's perspective.

1

The Data Base

Very little of the demographic data recorded on the pages that follow stems from my own original research into primary sources. The vast majority of the material examined and analyzed was the painstaking work of previous scholars and researchers. Thus, I am enormously indebted to fellow Sovietologists, historians, political scientists and, most especially, the research team that was part of the Munich-based Institute for the Study of the USSR (unfortunately, no longer in existence) and the present day researchers associated with Radio Free Europe/Radio Liberty.

The biographical work formerly done at the Institute and now carried on by RFE/RL researchers is an invaluable treasure trove of information about prominent Soviet personalities from Lenin and Gorky to Gorbachev and Solzhenitsyn. Those researchers have devoted thousands of hours pouring through Soviet publications. Whenever a name, date, notation about an individual's educational experience, career, etc. is found the data has been duly recorded and later published in such volumes as PROMINENT PERSONALITIES IN THE USSR (1968) or the 1984 compilation by Alexander G. Rahr, A BIOGRAPHIC DIRECTORY OF 100 LEADING SOVIET OFFICIALS. (1) Again, without the enormous contribution of the Institute and the RFE/RL researchers, anything that may be of empirical value here never could have been produced in the collective lifetimes of several individual scholars.

However, as indicated above, the data base is not built solely upon the findings of the Munich researchers. For example, their biographies do not include a note on Lazar Kaganovich's nationality. However, Roy Medvedev records that Kaganovich came from a "poor Jewish family." (2) Such sources, along with my own judgement, have been the base for making some few changes in, or additions to, the material presented in the biographies.

While most of the data dealt with is "hard" (e.g., dates of birth and the years of tenure on the Politburo), some of it is more subjective. Thus, some of the conclusions offered are, at least in part, dependent upon this analyst's judgement. For example, clearly Brezhnev left the Politburo because he died in office; Trotsky was expelled and many others left because they were summarily removed, if under less harsh circumstances. How about Khrushchev? Surely some will say, with truth, that he was removed by his colleagues. However, he was aging, and as discussed here, the evidence is that he went quietly. Therefore, this writer selected to list the primary cause of his removal as "health." I hope, where such judgement calls have been made my choices have erred on both ends of the spectrum and, therefore, have not seriously biased the findings in any one direction.

While not ignoring previous historical and political analysis of Kremlin politics, the present study attempts to reexamine existing knowledge through a systematic analysis of changing Politburo demographics as they have evolved from 1917 to the present.

A reasonable criticism might be raised that while major international events have not been totally ignored in my review of Politburo politics, they have been downplayed. However, a major premise of the study is that even in the Soviet Union the overwhelming major concern of top political leaders is with domestic events and problems. Thus, I submit that any understanding of the workings of the Soviet Politburo must rest largely on a dual knowledge of the mechanics of Soviet politics and internal priorities.

In his masterful and highly prophetic study of STALIN'S SUCCESSORS, Seweryn Bialer put it very well:

> I do not share the view of those who assign to Soviet foreign policy and international accomplishments an increasingly dominant role in legitimizing the regime and in achieving its stability. In my opinion the dominant sources of both Soviet legitimacy and stability, both for the population and the elite, are overwhelmingly domestic in nature. Internal factors are sufficient to explain the regime's legitimacy and stability. (3)

In his history of Soviet Russia Adam Ulam essentially makes the same point in his concluding chapter. As he states, after the early years when the leaders were preoccupied with thoughts of a world revolution they "transferred in time into politicians for whom the development and strengthening of the Soviet state took the first and overwhelming priority." (4)

There is another, very important point of view that I share with Bialer, which is that the "crisis of the 1980s" faced by the Soviet leaders is overwhelmingly economic in nature. Thus, economic problems, especially the declining rate of economic growth, is the focal point of the concluding chapter of his book. (5) This, also, is the focal point of my analysis, especially in the final chapters.

My approach was first to identify and catalogue all of the pertinent empirical data on the Politburo that I could find --e.g., its numbers, makeup, turnover, etc.-- for each year from 1917 to 1985. After having accumulated the data I concentrated on answering one key question. In light of previous knowledge of Soviet history and politics, what additional might be learned from an examination of the continuities and changes of the Politburo over the years?

In planning the study I accepted the widely held view that Soviet political history is best understood by dividing it into eras associated with the leadership style of the first secretaries of the CPSU who dominate the Soviet political scene during their tenure in office. Thus the major sections of the work are: "The Lenin Politburo: 1917-21," "The Stalin Era: 1922-52," "The Khrushchev Era: 1953-63," "The Brezhnev Era: 1964-81," "The Andropov-Chernenko Interregnum 1982-84," and "The Dawn of a Gorbachev Era: 1985-??"

However, Soviet history, supported by the empirical measures generated in the study, suggested very early that within most of the eras there are important sub-periods that need to be dealt with if the analysis is to help illuminate Politburo politics. For example, what primarily concerned the members of the Stalin Politburo during the early years of his stewardship (1922-26), when he was struggling for Lenin's mantle, was quite different from their concerns after 1926 when Stalin had emerged as the undisputed leader. Similarly, Politburo concerns during the war with Germany were radically different from the preoccupations of its members during the immediate post-war reconstruction period. With the above in mind I attempted to identify sub-periods within each of the eras.

How could the first years of these sub-periods be identified? The decision was to let the Politburo speak for itself through a measure of membership stability on that body. Thus the change-index was created.

The major assumption upon which this index rests is that once he has assumed the position of first secretary, a leader has the major say as to who enters or exits from that body. Of course, whether due to terminal illness, or a loss of confidence among his colleagues, this would not be true in the final year of a first secretary's incumbency.

As shown in Figure 1, the change-index was designed to show the extent of politically driven change over time. Since there is no fixed number of Politburo members, the index was calculated with data reflecting percentage change. The index (d) was calculated from the formula:

$$d = a + b - c$$

where, a = percent of new Politburo members in year t
b = percent of total members removed in year t-1
c = percent removed by death or ill health in year t-1

The relative change was measured with (a) and (b); they were combined in order to indicate the full measure of turnover --especially important since the size of the Politburo fluctuates. Members who left the Politburo because of ill health or death (c) were excluded from consideration since these cases probably would not figure into a first secretary's plans to achieve support for his policy changes by deliberately shifting personnel.

In order to make the index numbers more manageable and to reflect the fluctuation between stability and active change, the index was transformed by calculating residuals from a linear regression. Simply stated, the change index measures the relative degree of annual change made in the Politburo membership, and the trend for such change, excluding removal for health reasons. So constituted, the lower the score, the greater the stability of the Politburo; the higher the score, the less the stability.

The scores generated for all of the years range from a -21 in 1918, when there was total stability on the original Politburo, to a +101 in 1957, when Khrushchev presided over wholesale changes in the membership. More importantly, without ignoring Soviet history, indeed taking for granted that the ascension of a new leader to power marked the beginning of a new era, I used the index as the primary guide for identifying the first year of each of the subperiods since Stalin's appointment as first secretary in 1922.

FIGURE 1

POLITBURO CHANGE-INDEX

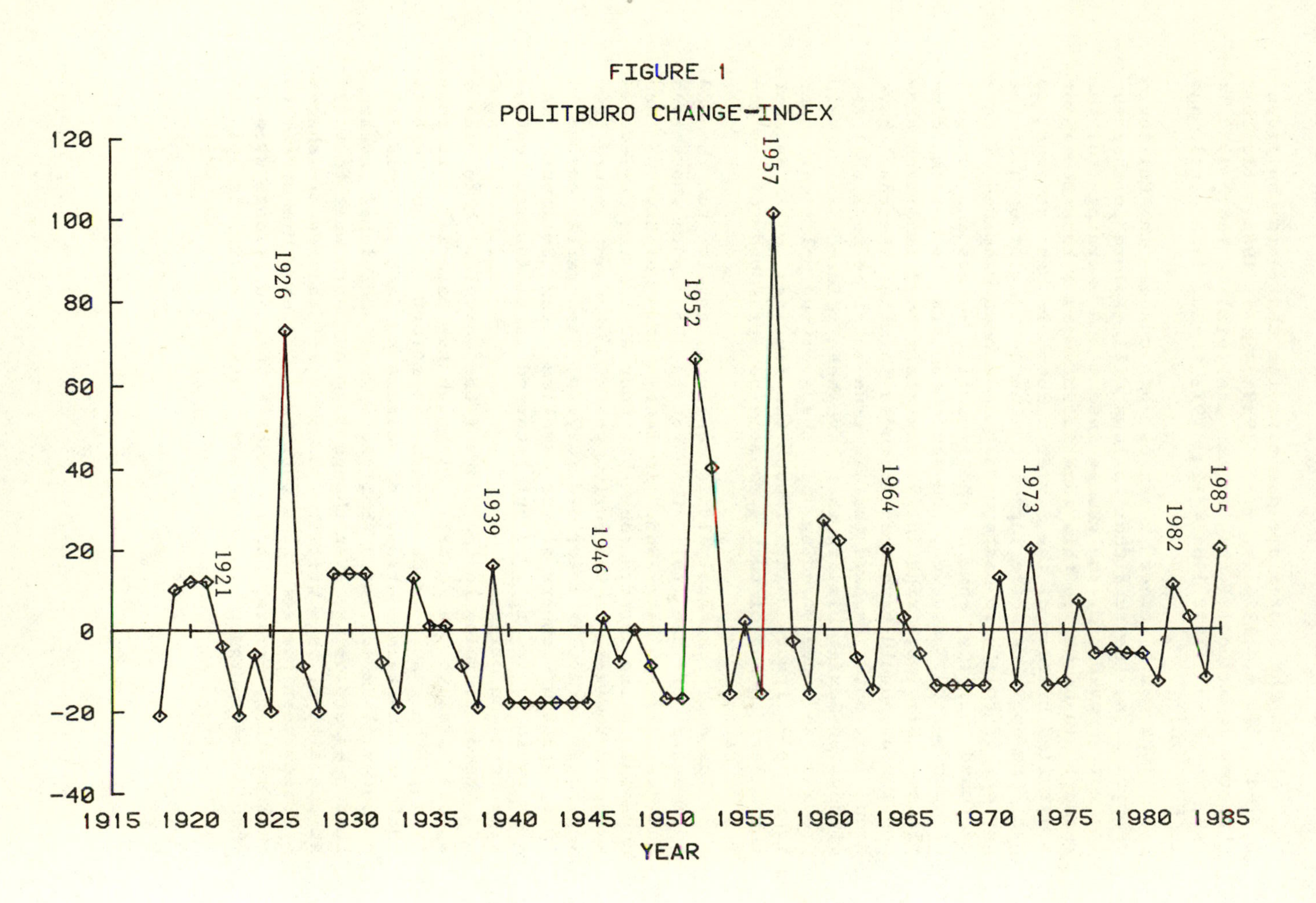

All of the scores are positive for the years so identified. Thus, 1926 = +73, 1939 = +16, 1946 = +3, 1952 (treated as a special case in the analysis) = +66, 1953 = +40, 1957 = +101, 1964 = +20, 1973 = +20, 1982 = +11, and 1985 = +20.

Along with other measures of change in Politburo demographics, the text that follows will explore further the insights provided by the change-index. A warning to the reader! In no way is this work intended as a substitute for a detailed history of the Soviet Union. In an attempt to put the empirical offerings into the setting of each of the periods of Politburo history that have been examined, I have sketched briefly some of the important events and concerns of each period. However, the sketches are far from complete. Critics, rightfully, may claim that important elements that should have been included in the sketches have been left out. Perhaps that is true but I do hope that the windows on Soviet history that have been offered will help provide an understanding of the evolving political scene from the Politburo down. I hope the findings will augment the understanding of that awesomely powerful body of men and its functions.

The empirical analysis is confined largely to the 89 incumbents of the full, thus voting, Politburo who served between 1917 and late-1985. In fact, only eighty-two men and one woman served on that body during the period examined. However, in the early years Zinov'yev served two separate terms, as later did Kosygin, temporarily ousted in 1952, and four members of the swollen 1952 Politburo who also were ousted in 1953 but returned later for more extensive terms in office.

Before turning to the body of the work I wish to make a special plea to the reader. Although the material that follows is the result of many months of effort, I am certain that it contains errors of judgement, fact and omission. Moreover, I am convinced that there are additional avenues that need exploring, even though I am not sure what they are at the time of this writing. However, if the reader shares my view that the effort is worthwhile, I urge him or her to tell me of my errors, and to suggest what additional avenues should be pursued in possible future revisions of the material.

KEY AND ABBREVIATIONS FOR PROFILES

Notes

a. Family background = worker if designated as such and/or born in an urban area (unless there is another designation) --i.e., intellectual = son of clergy, engineer, gentry, teacher or white collar, peasant = designation as such and/or born in a village.

b. Determined by designation or name and/or republic of birth.

c. Whether complete or incomplete.

d. Highest rank whether a political or career officer, also Cmdr = active leadership role in the fighting during the Revolution and/or the Civil War and/or in the fighting during World War II.

e. Whether first secretary of gorod, krai, oblast or first secretary of republic Party organization at the time of, or prior to, elevation to the Politburo.

f. The year(s) of entry into and the year(s) of exit from being an active candidate or full member of the Politburo --i.e., names listed as Politburo members only during a specific meeting of a Party congress have not been counted as members.

g. Held office in one or more of these organs at some point in their career.

h. Cause of death assumed natural unless other evidence, plus early death in prison = Ntrl?

Where there are blank spaces we assume that the biographies consulted would have included such data if it were pertinent.

Where we have found conflicting data (e.g., different dates of entery into the Politburo) in most cases we have used the data supplied in the most recent source. For computation purposes those listed in office during one year alone are counted as having been in office a full year (even though they may have served but several months), those in two years as two full years, etc.

In 1952 the name of the Politburo was changed to Presidium and the duties of the Orgburo and the Secretariat were combined. In 1966 the name Politburo was restored.

A question mark indicates author's estimate of a date, cause of death, etc.

Abbreviations

Acad = Academy
AgP = Agitation and Propagand Department
Ag = Agriculture
Amb = Ambassador
APG = Anti-Party Group
Arm = Armanian
B = Before --e.g., Before 1917 = B1917
Back = Backgound
Bel = Belorussia or Belorussian
Bols = Bolshevik Party
Cand = Candidate member of Politburo
CC CPSU = Central Committee Communist Party Soviet Union
Cheka = All-Russian Extraordinary Commission
Coll = College
Chmn = Chairman
ClG = Colonel General
CltMin = Minister of Culture
Cmdr = Played an active leadership role in the fighting in Revolution, Civil War or World War II
Cms = Commissar
CmsMA = Commissar for Military Affairs
CmsNts = Commissar of Nationalities
CommMin = Communications Minister
CPCC = Communist Party Control Committee
CStffA = Chief of Staff of Red Army
DfMin = Minister of Defense
Dip = Diplomat
DrMLI = Director Marxism-Leninism Institute
Ecn = Economics
Ed = Education
EdKom = Edited Kommunist
EdPrv = Edited Pravda
Eng = Engineer
Exec = Executed
Exl = Exiled
Exp = Exprience
Expl = Expelled
Fst = First or General Secretary of CPSU
Fst + name = First secretary of administrative unit
Hist = Historian
Fin = Finland

ForCms = Foreign Commissar = Foreign Minister in later years
ForMin = Foreign minister = Foreign Commissar in earlier years
Gen = General
Genis = Generalisimo
Georg = Georgia or Georgian
Gnt = Gentry
Gorod = City
Gos = Gosplan
Higher Ed = Higher education --i.e. at least some whether or not completed
Hist = Historian
ImPurg = Imprisoned during the 1930s purges
Inst = Institute of higher learning
Int = Intellectual
Hlth = Health (including age) --i.e., probable real reason for removal from office
KarFin = The former Karlo-Finish Republic
Kazak = Kazakh or Kazakhstan
Krai = Administrative region
Lat = Latvia or Latvian
Len = Leningrad
LtG = Lieutenant General
Lw = Law
Mil = Military
MilA = Military Academy
MjG = Major General
Mshl = Marshal of Soviet Union
Murd = Murdered
Lat = Latvia or Latvian
Nd = no data --e.g., not listed in biographies consulted
Ntrl = Natural cause of death --i.e., assumed natural unless there is evidence otherwise
Ntrl? = Unsure death cause was natural --e. g., died at an early age in prison
NtrlCa = Death from car accident
Oblast = Administrative region
Org = Orgbureau
Peas = Peasant
Ped = Pedological = Teacher training in institute
Pm = Served as Chairman Council of Ministers, thus Prime Minister
PolA = Political or Party Academy or School
Poly = Polytechnical or technical training
Pb = Politburo
POrg = Department for Party Organizational Work

Prof = University Professor

Prs = Served as Soviet head of state, thus the President

Purg = Arrested during 1930s purges

Rem = Removed and/or no known reason for removal

Russ = Russia or Russian

Sec = Secetary at republic or regional level or member CPSU CC Secretariat

Sect = Secretariat of the CPSU CC

Suic = Committed suicide

Teach = Teacher or Lecturer

Theo = Theological training

Travel = Travel outside of the Bloc since 1917

TU = Trade Union Leader

Ukrain = Ukraine or Ukrainian

Uzb = Uzbek or Uzbekistan

Wkr = Worker

Yes = Held one or more important central posts

NOTES

1. The biographical sources consulted are listed in the Bibliography.

2. Roy Medvedev, ALL STALIN'S MEN: SIX WHO CARRIED OUT THE BLOODY POLICIES, Garden City, New York: Anchor Press Doubleday, 1984, p. 114.

3. Seweryn Bialer, STALIN'S SUCCESSORS: LEADERSHIP STABILITY AND CHANGE IN THE SOVIET UNION, New York: Cambridge University Press, 1980, p. 157.

4. Adam B. Ulam, A HISTORY OF SOVIET RUSSIA, New York: Praeger Publishers, 1976, p 297.

5. Bialer, Op. Cit. p. 286.

2

The Qualitative Politburo Environment

Most of the material offered on the pages that follow depends upon quantitative measures of evolving Politburo affairs. However, I do not agree with those (like Lenin) who have argued that only things that can be counted and measured are important.

At best, the empirical findings will add some new insights into Politburo affairs that were not previously perceived by historical and political analysts. With that in mind, before looking at the empirical analysis, the reader needs to know the author's qualitative assessment of the Soviet political system and the role of the Politburo as the focal point of Soviet leadership. This section of the presentation will provide the reader with the perspective used by this analyst in weighing the empirical evidence offered here.

The first entry into any catalogue of Soviet politics must be an underscored notation that the USSR is an authoritarian system. The people that populated Tsarist Russia and their Soviet descendants have never known rule by law, only rule by man. Thus, since universally security is a prime desire of both individuals and societies as a whole, both the Russian and Soviet leaders and society at large have evinced a preference for strong leaders, "little fathers" who would do what is necessary to secure peace and tranquility, both domestically and abroad.

In the 1917 beginning, as has been the case ever since, those on the top were self-selected individuals who believed it was their right and duty to impose their vision of "truth" on society. Further, with the passage of time, they have replenished their ranks by coopting new members from below, out of the ranks of the Central Committee. Thus, while the vast majority of the members of the Central Committee wear other hats as key second-level Party and state officials, a major function of that body is to serve as a training ground and depository for the future leadership of the Party "vanguard," the "guardians" of society (a la Plato), from which future Politburo members are drawn.

Essential to understanding the pages that follow is a knowledge of how elections Soviet-style work, since at all levels elections are predetermined by the NOMENKLATURA system.

Theoretically, chairmen of collective farms, members of village soviets (councils) and members of the Supreme Soviet are elected by the appropriate electorate. Similarly, on the Party side of the hierarchy, new members are elected into the local Party group. Members of the Party congresses are elected from their regions by the Party members in those regions. In turn the Party congresses elect the several-hundred-member Central Committee of the Communist Party of the Soviet Union, and that body elects the Politburo, which then serves as the executive committee responsible for managing the day-to-day affairs of the Party.

Such elections are held. However, with rare exception (i.e., only at the lowest levels) the outcome is predetermined by the NOMENKLATURA. Always there is only one candidate and that person is the nominee of a higher Party group. Thus, for example, the nominee for the post of chairman of a collective farm is selected by the OBLAST (regional) Party committee. Similarly, this is the process by which new members of the Politburo are chosen.

The incumbent members of the Politburo have their NOMENKLATURA list of possible appointees to all high national offices (e.g., including the editorship of PRAVDA). Thus, when a new member is wanted for the Politburo, with the aid and advice of the Secretariat of the CPSU, the existing members nominate the person they wish to join them, and that individual is ratified at the next plenum of the Central Committee. As implied above, the nominees always have been drawn from the ranks of the Central Committee. (1)

Rooted in the above are a number of special attributes of Soviet society, quite different from Western democratic societies, that must be taken into account in any attempt to understand the Soviet leaders, especially the Politburo which is "responsible for everything." (2) (See Khrushchev's statement quoted in the epigraph to this study.)

In spite of Marxist-Leninist doctrinal statements to the contrary, in practice, the Soviet Union is the most state oriented of all societies. Virtually everyone works for the USSR Incorporated. Moreover, the intertwined state-party bureaucracies are not satisfied just with managing all economic affairs. The effort and intent is to penetrate every sphere of human experience. Thus, unlike presidents and prime ministers in the "open societies" of the West, Soviet leaders try to be "responsible for everything."

Western economists have dubbed the Soviet Union a "command economy." It is more than that. It is a command society, in which nothing is outside of the purview of the Politburo. To the degree that it is possible, the members of the Politburo attempt to engineer the whole of the citizens' lives. Unfortunately, the members of the Politburo are not gods. As a result of their inability to know and see everything they have been driven to establish priorities which, in practice, has meant that much of importance, especially to the ordinary citizens, is seriously neglected, because it never has a meaningful place on the Politburo's agenda.

To our knowledge, as yet, Gorbachev has not stated in any of his speeches that a major task of the USSR is building "the new Soviet man." However, if such a passage is not included in one of his future speeches, he will break precedent with those who have gone before him.

While the Politburo does not ignore public opinion, it does view popular aspirations and desires quite differently from the way politicians in multi-party systems view them. Votes are never counted by eager Soviet politicians concerned over their fate. Public pressure groups are not a prime consideration in assuring continued tenure in office. The goals and values of society are not prime political considerations that shape a Rousseauian "general will" that springs from the commonweal.

The members of the Politburo continuously spend much of their effort making speeches and writing tracts expressing their view of a Soviet common will, but always with the premise that Soviet values and goals are rooted in the Marxist-Leninist "science of society." Moreover, because the leaders are cognizant of the reality of change, current "truth" is the incumbent leaders' most recent interpretation of the holy writs, in ways that will best serve current needs. Again quoting Khrushchev, not only must the leaders "understand everything" but also they are responsible for "recognizing right from wrong and good from evil, supporting the right way and vanquishing the wrong way." (3) There is no Soviet Protestant ethic wherein the individual is ultimately responsible for his or her salvation. That determination, too, is the responsibility of the Party leadership.

How do the Kremlin leaders justify to themselves and society the awesome responsibility they claim? The answer came from the inventive genius of Lenin's mind. The attractive coin of democracy probably reached its greatest luster early in this century, and the desirability of clothing the Bolshevik experiment in that luster was irresistible. Thus, Lenin proclaimed that the operative principle of Soviet politics would be "democratic-centralism." Theoretically, all new policy proposals are open to free and public debate until the proper course has been decided upon. At that point, however, all debate is closed. What Lenin never explained explicitly is what has been key to practice. Even in those relatively few instances when the leadership has called for a public debate on policy innovation, the Party always has insisted on retaining a monopoly over setting the agenda, so that all that ever remains to be done in public is the final crossing of the t's and the dotting of the i's on matters already decided upon by the Kremlin. Key, of course, to the whole process is the Politburo's insistence that it is the ultimate judge of what is ideologically correct in a society where every word and deed must square with the Marxist-Leninist "science of society." Freedom is defined as the "perception of necessity," which Soviet philosophers explain means recognizing, and obeying, the Marxist-Leninist laws.

Clearly, leadership style has varied with the personality of the first secretaries. Nevertheless, whether one thinks of Lenin or Stalin, Khrushchev or Brezhnev, the first secretaries of the CPSU always are more than merely first among equals. Brezhnev may escape from being publicly tarnished with the brush of "the cult of the individual" but, especially in his latter years of rule, he came to be viewed as a near demigod.

Inescapably, top Soviet leaders, especially the Party first secretaries, are surrounded by sycophants. An unspoken, enormously important, part of the Soviet leadership chemistry is the fact that even though lesser Soviet mortals may assiduously avoid breaking any laws, no one in the USSR has tenure in his position. Failure to fulfill plans and, most important of all, failure to satisfy one's political superiors in the performance of duty is cause for instant demotion, dismissal or (especially in earlier times) even worse.

Private free economic enterprise is not only illegal in the USSR, but practicing it outside of the most restricted limits is a major sin for which violators often are executed. The major exception is allowing the peasants to sell private plot produce on the kolkhoz markets.

Ironically, in a sense, the USSR has to be one of the most laissez faire political leadership systems in the world. Constantly, the Politburo is allowed to "fix the rules of competition...etc.... as they please." (Webster) Under the NOMENKLATURA system, the members of the Politburo know that every citizen in Soviet society is a chess piece to be used, or sacrificed, at the leaders' will.

Closely tied to the above is the leaders' monopoly over all information, and the corollary to that awesome power: Politburo members almost never are subjected to public scrutiny, much less criticism, while in power. A Watergate incident that drove an American president from power, a Greenpeace scandal that shakes the foundation of a French government is unthinkable in the USSR. Such actions are normal, standard operating procedure in Soviet politics.

Aside from the possibility that the Politburo members might occasionally scan some illegal SAMIZDAT publications (i.e., underground, "self-edited," dissident tracts), the Politburo members are not subjected to the kind of domestic public criticism that is featured daily in the Western press concerning Western leaders.

Undoubtedly, unlike the ordinary citizens who only know what is in PRAVDA, IZVESTIA and the other official media sources (supplemented for some by RL, VOA and BBC broadcasts), the Kremlin leaders do receive their daily budget of translations from the Western press. Also, the top leaders have at hand all of the domestic information that for security reasons is not openly published (e.g., accounts of plane crashes, natural disasters, illegal strikes and, in recent years, the grain harvest figures, etc.). Nevertheless, when compared to the Western leaders' sources of information, indeed the sources available to the Western public at large, the Politburo's window on the world of knowledge is quite limited.

Whether or not one believes that "totalitarianism" (4) still best describes the Soviet system of rule, or that some other term, such as "monohierarchy" (5) or just plain authoritarianism is more accurate, Hannah Arendt eloquently described a major informational problem faced by the Politburo when she wrote:

> Practically speaking, the paradox of totalitarianism in power is that the possession of all instruments of governmental power and violence in one country is not an unmixed blessing for a totalitarian movement. Its disregard for facts, its strict adherence to the rules of a fictitious world, become steadily more difficult to maintain, yet remains as essential as before. Power means a direct confrontation with reality, and

totalitarianism in power is constantly concerned with overcoming this challenge. (6)

Without an investigative, critical press, university professors allowed to search for truth where they find it, and independent "think-tanks" which pursue their own independent interests on domestic matters, the Soviet leaders are almost totally dependent on the lower rungs of the bureaucracy when making policy decisions. Writing about a world before the dawn of the USSR, Max Weber put his finger on a major problem faced by the Politburo decision makers.

> The absolute monarch is powerless opposite the superior knowledge of the bureaucratic expert--in a certain sense more powerless than any other political head... When a constitutional king agrees with a socially important part of the governed, he very frequently exerts a greater influence upon the course of administration than does the absolute monarch. The constitutional king can control these experts better because of what is, at least relatively, the public character of criticism, whereas "the absolute monarch is dependent for information solely upon the bureaucracy." (7)

Ironically, the members of the Politburo may well be captors of the very bureaucracy that spawned them in the first place. Here, again, we see a price paid for a command system, wherein the leadership is forced to operate according to priorities. Since the Kremlin leaders cannot really be responsible for everything, much must be left to the regional and district officials (primarily the Party Secretaries) who are on the firing line. In short, as Alec Nove has put it: "Many commands are written by those who receive them." (8)

Overwhelmingly, as our empirical study documents, when most of the future Politburo members were young Party zealots, they first served as local Party or state functionaries. Some, very few, subsequently advanced through the ranks of just one or the other of the twin party-state hierarchies (e.g., Gromyko served almost entirely on the state side), but most climbed to and fro between party and state posts as they ascended the bureaucratic ladder. For example, early in their career many destined for the Politburo first headed an important local state or Party office, from whence they were promoted to be Party or state rayon (district) officials. After successfully serving at the rayon level, for most, the next step was to be promoted to the position of either oblast (regional) or republic first secretary. At that point the most successful were elevated to the rank of candidate member of the Politburo.

The importance of the fact that from early on in the Stalin years, the Politburo has been dominated by men whose ultimate rise to the top of Soviet power was determined by their mid-career success as Party prefects at the regional and republic level hardly can be exaggerated.

Taking their orders from Moscow, ultimately responsible only to the Kremlin, the Party prefects are the few thousand individuals who rule the society and the economy at the base level. There, on the firing line, the rules are quite clear. If the prefect's district, region, or republic fails to meet plan and, for example, it is clear to all that bad weather was responsible for a crop failure, the chances are that the rayon, or oblast, first secretary in the affected area will be retained in office. However, the price paid for political ambition in the USSR is that all failures attributable to human error are assumed to stem from poor or dishonest management, and the prefects are responsible for everything within their domain. Soviet policies and Politburo pronouncements are never wrong and never criticized as long as the incumbents remain in office. Sometimes even Moscow ministers are taken to task, but most of all the blame goes to the prefects, and serious human error is never forgiven.

Candidacy, a period of probation, is an open, operative practice for new Party members, new members of the Central Committee, and the majority of the Politburo inductees. In practice, but not in name, that same testing period is even more important for those who achieve prefectship, especially over a key region (e.g., Brezhnev's stewardship over the "new-lands" of Kazakhstan and Gorbachev's service as first secretary of Stavropol krai), with the hope for bigger and better things in the future. In sum, those relatively few individuals who pass the test with flying colors have demonstrated to their superiors that they fully fit the mold. They are suited to be placed upon the most important of the Soviet NOMENKLATURA lists, the one that contains the names that will be considered for a future place on the Politburo.

Inevitably, almost from the beginning, key to successful political advancement has been an in-built patron-client system. Part and parcel of successful advance under the NOMENKLATURA system has been the success of an individual to serve faithfully under a powerful superior. Thus, Suslov (1955-82), whose territorial base was Stavropol, is believed to have played an important role in the promotion of Gorbachev to the Politburo to be the Party's overseer of agriculture. (9)

Because, I believe, of a hope by some in the West that the USSR will evolve into a system more compatible with Western values, one often reads and hears that important changes surely will occur when a "new generation" of Soviet leaders take over in the Kremlin. Such hopes are rooted in an ignorance of the years of screening and testing that go into selecting new Politburo members. Of course, in some sense, there is a new generation of Politburo members.

Only Gromyko is old enough to remember the revolution. Most of the 1985 Politburo never met Stalin. In a few years, most of the members will know about World War II only from historical accounts. Gorbachev was only nine years old in 1940. But, Gorbachev and all of his colleagues have passed the supreme test. Before being asked to join the Politburo they proved to their seniors that they fully fit the mold from which all Politburo members come. True, there have been some evolutionary changes. Callous disregard for human life probably is no longer a positive attribute for Politburo candidacy, but most of the other attributes Stalin looked for in the men he brought on board remain the same.

Without contradicting his observation concerning the power of bureaucrats over authoritarian leaders, Weber recognized the other side of the coin. If the top leaders are astute and acknowledge the great power of the bureaucratic experts, leaders can wield the bureaucracy to achieve their desired ends. In his words:

> Bureaucracy is the means of carrying "community action" over into rationally ordered "societal action," therefore, as an instrument of "societalizing" relations of power, bureaucracy has been and is a power instrument of the first order --for the one who controls the bureaucratic apparatus. (10)

Stalin proved to be a master of the bureaucracy throughout most of his rule. Khrushchev successfully manipulated the bureaucracy during his early years in power. Brezhnev both used, and compromised with, the bureaucracy. History has yet to reveal how Gorbachev will deal with the Soviet "instrument of first order."

For Westerners to understand Politburo politics, they must use discretion when making comparisons between one system and another. There are important similarities between Western top cabinet members and Soviet Politburo members, but also there are significant differences. For example, in Western constitutional systems a sharp distinction is made between the permanent bureaucracy, responsible for executing laws and policies, and the elected or appointed politicians accountable to the electorate. A president's or prime minister's cabinet serves at that official's pleasure, but the permanent bureaucracy is protected by civil service guarantees. There is no concept of civil service in the USSR. There is no constitutional break between the Politburo policy makers and the lower officials who carry out the decision makers' policies. In sum, the Politburo is the top rung of an unbroken bureaucratic hierarchy that stretches from the Kremlin to the lowest factory foreman or state farm brigade leader.

In the Soviet Union, today's equivalent of a US G.S. 15 (a top level civil servant) someday might be elevated to Politburo status. For good or ill, success on even the highest rungs of a Western bureaucracy is not a stepping stone to the highest offices in the land.

Some who see parallels where they do not exist might equate Reagan's service as the Governor of California with Gorbachev's tenure as first secretary of Stavropol krai. There is no comparison. Reagan built his reputation on his success in being elected by the California voters. Gorbachev built his success as a successful regional administrator appointed to his post by higher authority.

Another special feature of Politburo rule that must be accounted for in understanding top Soviet policy making is that there is no legislature or independent court that must be answered to. From Lenin onward every proposal placed before the Supreme Soviet by higher administrative authorities (ultimately the Politburo) has been passed unanimously, often after actual implementation. Soviet courts help interpret the law, but never by challenging the authority of the lawmakers. This right is ultimately monopolized by the Politburo.

Finally, in this incomplete listing of special factors and forces that must influence Politburo thought and action, there is the Marxist-Leninist ideology. When they perceive it necessary, the Soviet leaders (adhering to a major Lenin dictum) have shown themselves to be highly pragmatic. Yet, at the very least Marxism-Leninism is both the lingua franca of Soviet political dialogue and the primary legitimizer for the leaders' actions. I believe that the ideology is more than that but, whatever the truth, no modern Western administration is made up of men who constantly solemnly swear that they adhere uniformly to the same unquestioned source of all truth.

When this writer reads or hears Western commentators unqualifiedly drawing parallels between Politburo politicians and top Western politicians (e.g., Carter and Brezhnev or Reagan and Gorbachev), he often becomes very concerned. Such parallels frequently confuse more than they enlighten. In sum, without a close knowledge of the peculiar environment within which the Politburo functions, one cannot really begin to understand how it works.

NOTES

1. Interestingly, the NOMENKLATURA is rarely openly discussed in the USSR. This writer has never seen it mentioned in books on Soviet government. Indeed, in this connection I had a bit of fun on one of our travels to the USSR during a visit to a collective farm. As is customary on such occasions, at the start of the visit the chairman addressed his visitors describing the farm and its successes. In response to a question from one of our group, the chairman proudly announced that he had served in his post for some twenty years, having been reelected several times by the farm members. At that point, I spoke up, congratulating him on his long tenure, and asking if it was not correct that under the NOMENKLATURA system originally he had been nominated by the regional Party committee. He and his staff were sitting on a platform at the front of the meeting room. They went into a private huddle, chatted among themselves for a couple of minutes, and then renewed the discussion by turning to another matter. My question was not answered.

2. N. S. Khrushchev, "Speech to Agricultural Workers at Gorky," SEL'SKOE KHOZYAISTVO, April 10, 1957, pp. 1 & 2.

3. Ibid.

4. If, as many believe, the term totalitarianism is inescapably linked with rule by mass terror, the term has not applied to the Soviet system since the early years of Khrushchev's rule. However, even under Gorbachev, there is the attempt by the Politburo to maximize control over everything through the central monopoly over all decision making and direction of the economy, police, politics, education, literature, etc.

5. Roy D. Laird. THE SOVIET PARADIGM: AN EXPERIMENT IN CREATING A MONOHIERARCHICAL POLITY, New York: The Free Press, 1970.

6. Hannah Arendt, THE ORIGINS OF TOTALITARIANISM, New York: Meridian Books Inc., 1959, pp. 391-392.

7. Max Weber, ESSAYS ON SOCIOLOGY (translated and edited by Hans Gerth and C. Wright), New York: Oxford University Press, 1961, pp. 196-244.

8. In private conversation.

9. Alexander G. Rahr, A BIOGRAPHIC DIRECTORY OF 100 LEADING SOVIET OFFICIALS, Munich, Radio Liberty, RFE/RL, August, 1984, p. 74.

10. Weber, Op. Cit., p. 228.

PART TWO

The Lenin-Stalin Years

Clearly, the two most distinct periods in the history of the Soviet Politburo are the Lenin-Stalin years 1917 though 1952 and the post-Stalin years 1953 to the present.

More than anything else the first period is marked by the struggle for the survival of a new system, both domestically and on the world scene. The victory of the Bolsheviks in the Civil War was hard won. The Kronstadt rebellion, discontent in the countryside and the famine of 1920-21 could have spelled the end of the Bolshevik experiment. Lenin was right: without the NEP retreat the new system may well have collapsed. Forced collectivization, Stalin's "revolution from above," could well have coalesced the peasant majority into a successful counter-revolution. Also, the mass purges could have precipitated serious opposition to Kremlin rule. Most of all, had Germany won World War II, there would be no Soviet system today, no Politburo that rules the vast Soviet empire from its Kremlin base. Whatever their faults, the Stalin Politburos did perform some remarkable deeds of leadership and system building.

3

Lenin's Politburo (1917–21)

By late summer 1917 there were some 240,000 members of the Russian Social-Democratic Labor Party of the Bolsheviks -- RSDRP(b). The Petrograd Sixth Congress, which was held at that time, had 157 voting and 110 "deliberative-vote" delegates. Thus, the number of chiefs had grown far too numerous to manage tribal affairs efficiently on a day-to-day basis, particularly if there was a plan afoot to take over the reins of government. As a result, the Central Committee, meeting October 23, 1917, "elected" a Political Bureau. (2)

The seven men elected October 23, 1917 presided over the 1917 Bolshevik coup d' etat. Their average age was 36.3 years. Lenin, the oldest, was 47. The youngest, Sokol'nikov, was only 29, while the rest were in their mid-thirties. From that time on there has been a gradual, and quite regular, increase in the average age, until a peak of 70 was reached in the early 1980s.

The original members of the 1917 Politburo and the years they served on that body were Bubnov (1917-19), Kamenev (1917-26), Lenin (1917-24), Sokol'nikov (1917-19), Stalin (1917-53), Trotsky (1917-26), and Zinov'yev (1917-20). Within three years, three of the original seven had been removed from power, while four new members had been added.

Aside from Lenin and Stalin, the other five members of the original 1917 Politburo were purged. Two were executed. Trotsky was murdered in Mexico and the other two died in prison.

Profile 1, "The Lenin Politburo: 1917-21," lists the 10 full and one candidate members who served under Lenin from 1917 through 1921. Aside from Stalin, all but Kalinin (1925-46) were gone by 1929. Kalinin, of course, was a Stalin full-voting appointee. Indeed, all but Kalinin (and of course Lenin) were destroyed in the forthcoming Stalin purge.

Profile 1
THE LENIN POLITBURO, 1917-1921*

a Family Back.	b Nation- ality	Year into Party	c Higher Ed.	d Military Exp.	e Repub. or Region 1st Sec	f Years Cand. Politburo or Presid.	f Years Full Politburo or Presid.
FULL VOTING MEMBERS							
BUBNOV, Andrey Sergeyevich, 1883-1940							
Wkr?	Russ	1905	Ag	Cmdr	----	----	1917-1919?
KAMENEV, Lev Borisovich, 1883-1936							
Int	Jewish	1901	Univ	----	----	1926-1927	1917-1926
LENIN, Vladimir Il'ich, 1870-1924							
Int	Russ	1898	Lw	----	----	----	1917-1924
SOKOL'NIKOV, Grigoriy Yakovlevich, 1888-1939							
Wkr?	Russ	1905	Lw/ecn	Cmdr	----	1924-1925	1917-1919?
STALIN, Iosif Vissarionovich, 1879-1953							
Wkr	Georg	1898	Theo	Genis	----	----	1917-1953
TROTSKY, Lev Davidovich, 1879-1940							
Int	Jewish	1902?	Coll	CmsMA	----	----	1917-1926
ZINOV'YEV, Grigoriy Yevseyevich, 1883-1936							
Wkr?	Russ	1903	Univ	----	Gorod	----	1917-1920 1924-1926
KRESTINSKIY, Nikolay Nikolayevich, 1888-1938							
Wkr?	Russ	1907?	Lw	----	Oblast	----	1919-1920
BUKHARIN, Nikolay Ivanovich, 1888-1938							
Int	Russ	1906	Ecn	----	----	1919-1920	1920-1929
PREOBRAZHENSKIY, Yevgeniy Alekseyevich, 1886-1937							
Int	Russ	1904?	----	----	----	----	1920-1921?
SEREBRYAKOV, Leonid Petrovich, 1890-1937							
Wkr	Russ	1912?	----	Cmdr	----	----	1920-1921?
CANDIDATE MEMBER ONLY DURING THE PERIOD							
KALININ, Mikhail Ivanovich, 1875-1946							
Peas	Russ	1898	----	----	----	1919-1926?	1926-1946?

* The key to the profile categories, including an explanation of the abbreviations used, can be found on pages 9-12.

g Sect. or Org.	g Pres- sidium Sup. Sov.	g Council of Ministers	Other Important Experience	Travel Outside Bloc	Why Off Politb.	h Cause of Death
Yes	----	----	Purg	----	Expl	Ntrl?
----	Prs	----	Impurg	Some	Expl	Exec
Fst	----	Pm	Founded Bols	----	Died	Ntrl
----	----	Yes	Gos. Impurg	----	Expl	Ntrl?
Fst	Yes	Pm	CmsNts	----	Died	Ntrl
Yes	----	Yes	CmsMA ForCms	Much	Expl	Murd
----	Yes	----	Impurg	----	Rem Expl	Ntrl Exec
Yes	----	----	Impurg	----	Expl	Exec
----	----	----	EdPrv Impurg	Some	Expl	Exec
Yes	----	----	Impurg	----	Expl	Ntrl?
Yes	----	Yes	Impurg	Little	Expl	Exec
----	Prs	----	----	----	Hlth	Ntrl

With the exception of Beriya who was executed in 1953, since the end of the Stalin era no former Politburo member has been either expelled in great shame or executed. A comparison of key demographic measures of the 1985 Politburo with the means for the 1917-21 body reveals other important differences in the nature and composition of the 13-man 1985 Politburo and that of the men who dominated the Bolshevik experiment in the early years (Table 1). Much of the discussion in the pages that follow will be devoted to an analysis of the importance of the changes which occurred between 1917 and 1985.

Little imagination is required to surmise what matters must have occupied almost all of the time and effort of the original Lenin Politburo. First, the "shameful" provisions of the Brest-Litovsk treaty had to be accepted if the fighting was to be stopped. The few weeks' breathing space afforded by the "Honeymoon of the Revolution," which occurred early in 1918 before the onset of the Civil War, did allow some dreaming about what the new society might be like --e.g., all the land had been nationalized, wages had been equalized, and military rank had been abolished. However, the Civil War accompanied by the allied interventions quickly turned all attention to doing what was necessary to save the Bolshevik experiment.

No sooner was the Civil War successfully completed when the Kronstadt Rebellion in 1921 punctuated messages Lenin had been receiving from the countryside that the peasants were very dissatisfied with the new order. As Lenin earlier had had to use all of his considerable persuasive abilities to convince the other members of the Politburo that Brest-Litovsk was necessary, now he had to concentrate his energies on persuading his colleagues that a New Economic Policy was essential --i.e., a retreat from building communism in the countryside, thus a "peasant Brest-Litovsk."

During Lenin's rule very little time could be devoted to system building, if indeed a new state was to rise out of the Tsarist phoenix.

Table 1

COMPOSITE MEASURES OF MEANS OF POLITBURO PERIODS: 1917-21 AND 1985*

	1917-21	1985
Number on Politburo	6	13
The change-index	+3	+20
% off from previous year (a)	3	18
% off health reasons (b)	0	9
% new (c)	4	23
Age Frst. Sec. first year	47	54
Politburo means		
Age	38	66
Total years served (d)	2	6
Origins in %		
Peasant	0	23
Worker	44	62
Intellectual	56	15
Russian	54	62
Ukrainian	0	15
Other Nationality	46	23
Education in %		
Some higher	80	54
Polytechnical	0	46
Experience in %		
Regional Frst. Sec.	12	54
Republic Frst. Sec.	0	15
Apprenticeship (e)	7	77
Secretariat or Orgburo	65	31
Presidium Sup. Sov.	41	23
Council of Ministers	58	46
Travel outside Bloc (f)	43	46

*The 1985 data is the mean for that year, for the other years the data is the mean for all of the years in the period.

a-The percentage of the previous year's Politburo that is not returned, b-the percentage of the previous year's Politburo not returned for health reasons, c-the percentage of that year's Politburo that is new, d-years served at that point in time, e-previous service either as a candidate or full Politburo member, f-excluding travel prior to 1917.

NOTES

1. In most cases, the time periods offered here, upon which the computations were made, count an individual in the Politburo the year of entry and off the Politburo during the year of exit. Fortunately, and one reason we decided on this method of eliminating overlapping is that most plenary and full sessions of the Central Committee have occurred early in the years they were held. Thus, for example, the Lenin Politburo is dated 1917-1921 because Stalin took over as first secretary early in 1922.

2. Crowley, E. L., Lebed, A. I. and Schulz, H. E. (Eds.). PARTY AND GOVERNMENT OFFICIALS OF THE SOVIET UNION 1917-1967, Metuchen, New Jersey: The Scarecrow Press, Inc., 1969, pp. 12 & 3.

4

The Stalin Era (1922–52)

Stalin Comes to the Forefront (1922-1925)

The onset of Lenin's debilitating, and ultimately fatal, illness resulted in Stalin's elevation to the post of first secretary in 1922, when only four (including Lenin and Stalin) of the original members remained. Moreover, between 1919 and 1922, five new members were added, although two would last only a year. The five were Krestinskiy (1919-20), Bukharin (1920-29), Preobrazensky (1920-21), Serebryakov (1920-21), and Tomsky (1922-29).

The Civil War had been successfully ended. The NEP was in place and destined to revive the enormously depressed levels of agricultural production. But the cold (from lack of adequate fuel) and hunger that had stalked Russia since mid-World War I now became even more acute. Famine swept much of the countryside at the start of the 1920s. Moreover, the debate over the proper path to the future still raged.

Some believed that Communism could not be built in one country and/or that predominantly peasant and agricultural Russia was not a base upon which such an edifice could be built. The "spark" and "permanent revolution" ideas dominated much thinking, especially Trotsky's. In the minds of such individuals the real raison d' etat for Bolshevism was to further the world revolution. Perhaps the Bolshevik coup would spark a genuine communist revolution in industrialized and proletarianized Western Europe which, subsequently, would serve to bring backward Russia along.

Increasingly, of course, such considerations as the above provided fuel for the struggle between Stalin and Trotsky for Lenin's mantle.

The period 1922-25 was the first of the interregnums marked by confusion at the top that is characteristic of

Politburo politics at the time of leadership transition. Although the Soviet Union has a constitution, and the Communist Party of the Soviet Union (CPSU) has its rules, in practice the laws and rules are ignored when a first secretary is fatally ill. Indeed, at all times the ultimate judgement as to what is law and what is to be done rests upon the most recent pronouncement emanating from the Politburo, especially the words of the first secretary. Thus, when he becomes totally incapacitated, the first secretary's Politburo colleagues are left to their own Byzantine devices. This was especially true between 1922 and 1924. As long as Lenin, whom Stalin was to transform into a Soviet God, lived a pall of uncertainty hung over the Kremlin, and no one, including Stalin, dared take important initiatives. Thus, most of the period was an interregnum of Soviet rule. Similarly, as discussed below, much of 1952 and 1953 was marked by indecision and inaction as was also the period from 1982 until 1985 when the Soviet Union lost three first secretaries in quick succession. In the latter period, neither Andropov nor Chernenko had time to line up the Politburo votes to institute whatever programs or policies they may have had in mind.

Lenin's second stroke in 1923 totally incapacitated him and he died in 1924. That same year Zinoviev was returned to the Politburo for a brief second term (1924-26) and Rykov (1924-30) was added to the body.

As the changing demographics illuminate, by the end of 1924 the battle for Lenin's mantle centered on Stalin and Trotsky. They were the only surviving members of the original seven. Hindsight, plus the demographics, support a conclusion that in that year Stalin achieved the dominant position on the Politburo. Beyond his ruthless ability to manipulate his colleagues, and the fact that he also held key positions on both the Orgburo and Secretariat, which played key roles in leadership selection and placement, by 1924 he had two other major factors in his favor. He had been first secretary for two years, and since he held that position when Zinoviev reentered and Rykov entered that body, those two men must have felt more beholden to Stalin than to Trotsky.

Profile 2, "The Stalin Politburo: 1922-25," records the demographic profile of the members who served under Stalin from 1922 through 1925.

Given the knowledge about that period in Soviet history, the numbers support an argument that by 1924 Stalin had won everything but the war. Surely, our understanding of Politburo politics, plus the dynamics of the demographic changes which were to occur in 1926, will challenge the conventional wisdom that Stalin did not secure himself fully in power until 1928.

Building the Stalinist System (1926-38)

Not only was Stalin able to have Trotsky expelled from the Politburo in 1926, but four new members were coopted into that body that year: Kalinin (1926-46), Molotov (1926-57), Rudzutak (1926-32) and Voroshilov (1926-60). Excluding Kalinin, who was 51, the average age of the other new members was 40, whereas that of the incumbents was 44. Given the advantage of hindsight, knowledge of the years those men were to remain in office suggests that they must have been acutely aware that their most important asset for survival was loyalty to Stalin. (1) Even including Rudzutak, who was later to commit fatal errors and be expelled, the average tenure in office of the four 1926 Stalin appointees was 22.8 years, in contrast with the average tenure of the Lenin Politburo (1917-22), excluding Stalin (35 years), which was only 4.1 years and of all the other members, besides Stalin, who have come and gone between 1917-1985, which is only 8.2 years.

Again, if one calculates the number of years served on the Politburo for each Politburo incumbent who has completed his term for each Politburo year 1917-1985, by far the biggest change in the average length of tenure (excluding the change between 1953 and 1954, because, as discussed in detail below, in 1953, 14 of the 16 members of the "extraordinary class of 1952" were absent in 1954) occurred between 1925 and 1926. The mean career tenure of the 1925 incumbents was seven years, whereas the mean tenure of the 1926 membership jumped to 16 years (Table 2).

Thus, with the exception of Bukharin and Tomsky (1922-29) the 1926 members (besides Stalin) surely recognized that the essential ingredient for survival was loyalty to Stalin. (2) All of the eleven earliest members of the Politburo (excluding Stalin and Lenin) were to be caught in the purges, six of whom were to be executed, one (Trotsky) was murdered, one committed suicide and the other three died at early ages while in prison.

Profile 2
THE STALIN POLITBURO, 1922-1925*

a Family Back.	b Nation-ality	Year into Party	c Higher Ed.	d Military Exp.	e Repub. or Region 1st Sec	f Years Cand. Politburo or Presid.	f Years Full Politburo or Presid.
FULL VOTING MEMBERS							
KAMENEV, Lev Borisovich, 1883-1936							
Int	Jewish	1901	Univ	----	----	1926-1927	1917-1926
LENIN, Vladimir Il'ich, 1870-1924							
Int	Russ	1898	Lw	----	----	----	1917-1924
STALIN, Iosif Vissarionovich, 1879-1953							
Wkr	Georg	1898	Theo	Genis	----	----	1917-1953
TROTSKY, Lev Davidovich, 1879-1940							
Int	Jewish	1902?	Coll	CmsMA	----	----	1917-1926
BUKHARIN, Nikolay Ivanovich, 1888-1938							
Int	Russ	1906	Ecn	----	----	1919-1920	1920-1929
TOMSKY, Mikhail Pavlovich, 1880-1936							
Wkr	Russ?	1904	----	----	----	----	1922-1929
RYKOV, Aleksey Ivanovich, 1881-1938							
Wkr?	Russ	1902	Lw	Cmdr	----	----	1924-1930
ZINOV'YEV, Grigoriy Yevseyevich (Reentry), 1883-1936							
Wkr?	Russ	1903	Univ	----	Gorod	----	1917-1920 1924-1926
CANDIDATE MEMBERS ONLY DURING THE PERIOD							
KALININ, Mikhail Ivanovich, 1875-1946							
Peas	Russ	1898	----	----	----	1919-1926?	1926-1946?
MOLOTOV, Vyacheslav Mikhaylovich, 1890-							
Peas	Russ	1906	Poly	----	----	1924?-1926	1926-1957
RUDZUTAK, Yan Ernestovich, 1887-1938							
Peas	Lat?	1905	----	----	----	1924?-1926 1934-1937	1926-1932
DZERZHINSKIY, Feliks Edmundovich, 1877-1926							
Int	Polish?	1905?	----	Cmdr	----	1924-1926	----

* The key to the profile categories, including an explanation of the abbreviations used, can be found on pages 9-12.

g Sect. or Org.	g Pres- sidium Sup. Sov.	g Council of Ministers	Other Important Experience	Travel Outside Bloc	Why Off Politb.	h Cause of Death
----	Prs	----	Impurg	Some	Expl	Exec
Fst	----	Pm	Founded Bols	----	Died	Ntrl
Fst	Yes	Pm	CmsNts	----	Died	Ntrl
Yes	----	Yes	CmsMA ForCms	Much	Expl	Murd
----	----	----	EdPrv Impurg	Some	Expl	Exec
----	-----	Yes	TU Purg	----	Expl	Suic
Yes	----	Pm	Impurg MVD	----	Expl	Exec
----	Yes	----	---- Impurg	----	Rem Expl	---- Exec
----	Prs	----	----	----	Hlth	Ntrl
Yes	Yes	Pm	ForMin	Much	Expl	----
----	Yes	Yes	Impurg	Some	Expl	Ntrl?
Yes	----	----	Cheka	----	Expl	Exec?

Profile 2
THE STALIN POLITBURO, 1922-1925 (Continued)

a Family Back.	b Nation-ality	Year into Party	c Higher Ed.	d Military Exp.	e Repub. or Region 1st Sec.	f Years Cand. Politburo or Presid.	f Years Full Politburo or Presid.
FRUNZE, Mikhail Vasil'yevich, 1885-1925							
Wkr	Ukrain?	1904	Poly	CStffA	----	1924-1925	----

g Sect. or Org.	g Pres. sidium Sup. Sov.	g Council of Ministers	Other Important Experience	Travel Outside Bloc	Why Off Politb.	h Cause of Death
----	----	----	CStffA	----	Died	Ntrl

Table 2

MEAN TENURE OF POLITBURO INCUMBENTS: KEY YEARS
(excluding Stalin)

1917	1925	1926	1917-85
4.1	7	16	8.6

Demographic comparisons between the Lenin Politburo (1917-21) and the Stalin Politburo in 1927 reveal some important changes. Among the eleven men who served under Lenin 1917-21, six came from worker homes, while five were reared in intellectual homes. Eight were Russians, two were Jewish and one, Stalin, was a Georgian. Also, eight had at least some higher education. In contrast, among the nine on the Stalin 1927 Politburo, three came from worker homes, two from an intellectual environment and four from peasant families. Seven were Russians, none were Jewish and there was one Georgian and one Latvian. By then only three had had at least some higher education. When some of the differences are expressed in percentage terms, some of the contrasts are striking (Table 3).

Table 3

STALIN VS. LENIN POLITBURO DEMOGRAPHICS
(in %)

	1917-21	1927
Workers	55	33
Intellectual	45	22
Peasant	0	44
Russian	73	78
Jewish	18	0
Other	9	22
Higher Ed.	73	33

This period, of course, is marked by the Stalin purges. Yet, an examination of the demographics of that awful event also supports a contention that Stalin was in full power by at least 1926. Including Trotsky who had been exiled before the major onset of the purges, 13 of the 25 men who served on the Politburo between 1917 and 1938 were caught in the purges: seven were executed and the other six died in prison. However, only three of those caught in the purges were among the 12 Stalin appointees between 1926 and 1938, and none of the three was executed, as far as we know, although they did die in prison at an early age. Put in other terms, whereas 65% of the members prior to 1926 were purged, only 25% of those appointed between 1926 and 1938 suffered such a fate. Thus, from 1926 on, most of the members of the Politburo were Stalin's accomplices rather than his victims in the continued scourge, which now concentrated on lower level officialdom, the army, and the kulaks.

As shown in Profile 3, "The Stalin Politburo: 1926-38," the fate of the individuals Stalin brought on board only as candidate members during the period was quite the opposite of those given full voting rights. All six of the individuals who served merely as candidate members from 1926 through 1938 were expelled. Two were executed and three died at an early age while in prison.

Although Stalin's practice was not to unveil his plans until he felt the time was ripe, one can suspect that he had decided upon the course he wanted to follow by the time he had ascended to full power.

In defeating Trotsky, Stalin's key tactic had been first to use the support and ideas of those on the right against him, but then when the left opposition was removed, he stole some of their concepts to defeat the right opposition. Trotsky had championed moving against the kulaks; when he was gone, Stalin massively moved to capture the rural means of production and, thus, the peasants. The majority of the population was peasant. Overwhelmingly, agriculture was the Soviet Union's major economic activity. He launched forced collectivization, his "revolution from above."

Although the executions, murders, and an awful man-made famine (rooted in the dislocation of cultivation) that accompanied forced collectivization cost upwards from five-million lives by the mid-1930s, Stalin had captured the peasants in the kolkhozy (collective farms) and sovkhozy (state farms). Moreover, in so doing he had effectively destroyed the kulaks who, had they survived, surely would have been central to any future rural opposition to central rule.

Capturing agriculture allowed Stalin to drain off rural resources to the cities for urban industrial construction. "All priority to industry" became the "first commandment" of Stalinist economic policy.

Profile 3
THE STALIN POLITBURO, 1926-1938*

a Family Back.	b Nation- ality	Year into Party	c Higher Ed.	d Military Exp.	e Repub. or Region 1st Sec.	f Years Cand. Politburo	f Years Full or Presid.
FULL VOTING MEMBERS							
STALIN, Iosif Vissarionovich, 1879-1953							
Wkr	Georg	1898	Theo	Genis	----	----	1917-1953
BUKHARIN, Nikolay Ivanovich, 1888-1938							
Int	Russ	1906	Ecn	----	----	1919-1920	1920-1929
TOMSKY, Mikhail Pavlovich, 1880-1936							
Wkr	Russ?	1904	----	----	----	----	1922-1929
RYKOV, Aleksey Ivanovich, 1881-1938							
Wkr?	Russ	1902	Lw	Cmdr	----	----	1924-1930
KALININ, Mikhail Ivanovich, 1875-1946							
Peas	Russ	1898	----	----	----	1919-1926?	1926-1946?
MOLOTOV, Vyacheslav Mikhaylovich, 1890-							
Peas	Russ	1906	Poly	----	----	1924?-1926	1926-1957
RUDZUTAK, Yan Ernestovich, 1887-1938							
Peas	Lat?	1905	----	----	----	1924?-1926 1934-1937	1926-1932
VOROSHILOV, Kliment Yefremovich, 1881-1969							
Peas	Russ	1903	----	Mshl	----	----	1926-1960
KUYBYSHEV, Valerian Vladimirovich, 1888-1935							
Int	Russ	1904	Lw	Cmdr	----	----	1927-1935
KAGANOVICH, Lazar Moissevich, 1893-							
Peas	Jewish	1911	----	Cmdr	Ukrain	1927-1930	1930-1957
KOSIOR, Stanislav Vikent'yevich, 1889-1939							
Wkr	Polish	1907	----	Cmdr	Ukrain	1927-1930	1930-1939?
ORDZHONIKIDZE, Grigoriy Konstantinovich, 1886-1937							
Peas	Gorg?	1907	----	Cmdr	Krai	1926-1930	1930-1937
ANDREEV, Andrei Andreevich, 1895-1971							
Peas	Russ	1914	----	----	----	1927-1934	1934-1952?

* The key to the profile categories, including an explanation of the abbreviations used, can be found on pages 9-12.

g Sect. or Org.	g Pres- siduium Sup. Sov.	g Council of Ministers	Other Important Experiencce	Travel Outside Bloc	Why Off Politb.	h Cause of Death
Fst	Yes	Pm	CmsNts	----	Died	Ntrl
----	----	----	EdPrv Impurg	Some	Expl	Exec
----	----	Yes	TU Purg	----	Expl	Suic
Yes	----	Pm	Impurg MVD	----	Expl	Exec
----	Prs	----	----	----	Hlth	Ntrl
Yes	Yes	Pm	ForMin	Much	Expl	----
----	Yes	Yes	Impurg	Some	Expl	Ntrl?
Yes	Prs	Yes	----	Some	Hlth	Ntrl
Yes	----	Yes	Gos	----	Died	Ntrl
Yes	----	Yes	APG	----	Expl	----
Yes	Yes	----	Impurg	----	Expl	Ntrl?
Yes	----	Yes	----	----	Died	Suic
Yes	Yes	Yes	Ag TU	----	Rem	Ntrl

Profile 3
THE STALIN POLITBURO, 1926-1938 (Continued)

a Family Back.	b Nation-ality	Year into Party	c Higher Ed.	d Military Exp.	e Repub. or Region 1st Sec.	f Years Cand.	f Years Full
						Politburo or Presid.	
KIROV, Sergey Mironovich, 1886-1934							
Wkr?	Russ	1904	Eng	Cmdr	Gorod	1927-1934	1934-1934
CHUBAR, Vlas Yakovlevich, 1891-1939							
Peas	Ukrain?	1904?	Poly	Cmdr	Ukrain	1927-1935	1935-1937?
MIKOYAN, Ansastas Ivonovich, 1895-1978							
Peas	Arm	1915	Theo	----	Krai	1926-1935	1935-1966
CANDIDATE MEMBERS ONLY DURING THE PERIOD							
KAMENEV, Lev Borisovich, 1883-1936							
Int	Jewish	1901	Univ	----	----	1926-1927	1917-1926
PETROVSKIY, Grigoriy Ivanovich, 1878-1958							
Wkr	Ukrain	1897	----	Cmdr	Ukrain	1926-1939	----
UGLANOV, Nikolay Aleksandrovich, 1886-1940							
Peas	Russ	1907	----	----	Gorod	1927-1929	----
POSTYSHEV, Pavel Petrovich, 1887-1940							
Wkr	Ukrain	1907?	----	Cmdr	Oblast	1934-1935	----
EYKHE, Robert Indrikovich, 1890-1940							
Peas	Lat	1911?	----	Cmdr	Krai	1935-1937?	----
YEZHOV, Nikolay Ivanovich, 1895-1939							
Wkr?	Russ?	1917	----	Gen	----	1937-1938?	----

g Sect. or Org.	g Pres- sidium Sup. Sov.	g Council of Ministers	Other Important Experience	Travel Outside Bloc	Why Off Politb.	h Cause of Death
Yes	Yes	----	----	----	Died	Murd
----	----	----	ImPurg	----	Expl	Ntrl?
----	Prs	Yes	----	Much	Hlth	Ntrl
----	Prs	----	Impurg	Some	Expl	Exec
----	Yes	----	----	----	Expl	Ntrl
Yes	----	Yes	Impurg	----	Expl	Ntrl?
----	Yes	----	Impurg	----	Expl	Ntrl?
----	----	Yes	Ag Impurg	----	Expl	Ntrl?
Yes	----	Yes	Impurg MVD Gen	----	Expl	Exec?

Why did he destroy the kulaks (the most productive of all the peasants), bloodily purge the Party of any real, or imagined, opposition, and decimate the army officer corps, especially at a time when his apologists claim that he already perceived the eventual German attack?

I believe that, consciously or unconsciously, Stalin was convinced that building the future required fashioning the "new Soviet man."

Whatever Stalin's motivations, he ruthlessly destroyed the most "inner-directed" members of society who through their genes, the kind of home environment they would have provided for their offspring, and their actions would have been the most likely source of resistance to Stalin's programs. (3) At that time, much of his vision of the future was revealed in such documents as the programatic Stalin Constitution of 1936 and the 1935 "Model Charter for Agricultural Artels," which became the basic law for the kolkhozy.

In large part those who survived the implantation of Stalinism were the "other-directed" members of society who were duly harnessed to a system that demanded them to sacrifice both themselves and the next generation to building Stalin's version of "socialism in one state."

Since Stalin's primary goal was to build a new and different society by weeding out all potential sources of opposition while expanding the industrial base as rapidly as possible, specific leadership qualities were required that were importantly different from those that had served successfully to consumate the revolution and Civil War. Indeed, beyond the differences in origins and educational background between the 1917-21 Lenin Politburo and the 1926-38 Stalin Politburo, there were some very important differences in the realm of leadership experience prior to Politburo status. Table 4 compares demographic measures of the 1917-21, 1922-25 and 1926-38 Politburos.

Among the 13 individuals who served on the Lenin and Stalin Politburos prior to 1926, only four (30%) had seen substantial action on the front during the Civil War. In contrast, among the 12 Stalin inductees during the years 1926 through 1938, six (54%) had had such leadership experience.

Table 4

COMPOSITE MEASURES OF MEANS OF POLITBURO PERIODS: 1917-38*

	1917-21	1922-25	1926-38
Number on Politburo	6	7	9
The change-index	+3	-13	+4
% off from previous year (a)	3	4	10
% off health reasons (b)	0	4	2
% new (c)	4	8	14
Age Frst. Sec. first year	47	43	47
Politburo means			
Age	38	43	47
Total years served (d)	2	4	6
Origins in %			
Peasant	0	0	63
Worker	44	45	27
Intellectual	56	55	10
Russian	54	54	56
Ukrainian	0	0	2
Other Nationality	46	46	52
Education in %			
Some higher	80	69	15
Polytechnical	0	0	13
Experience in %			
Regional Frst. Sec.	12	7	10
Republic Frst. Sec.	0	0	17
Apprenticeship (e)	7	15	63
Secretariat or Orgburo	65	46	72
Presidium Sup. Sov.	41	31	70
Council of Ministers	58	62	74
Travel outside Bloc (f)	43	46	35

*Means for all of the years within each of the periods.

a-The percentage of the previous year's Politburo that is not returned, b-the percentage of the previous year's Politburo not returned for health reasons, c-the percentage of that year's Politburo that is new, d-years served at that point in time, e-previous service either as a candidate or full Politburo member, f-excluding travel prior to 1917.

Among the individuals on the Politburo prior to 1926, only two (15%) had served as Party first secretaries of important regional areas (i.e., first secretaries of gorods, krais or oblasts) and none had served as republic first secretaries. Among the 12 Stalin appointees during the period, six (50%) served, or had served, as regional or republic first secretaries at the time of their induction on the Politburo. Further, in this connection, from 1926 on in most years individuals who were, or had been, first secretaries of the Leningrad and Moscow regions, and who had been, or still were, first secretaries of Belorussia, Georgia, the Ukraine or the Russian republic had served on the full Politburo or as candidate members. Moreover, since the opening of the new lands Kazakhstan has been so "represented." Finally, in recent years, most of the time the Foreign Minister, the Defense Minister and the head of the KGB has been either a full or candidate member of the Politburo.

As Bialer points out, since Khrushchev the general rule has been that "all major specialized hierarchies of the Soviet party-state have their chief executive represented on the Politburo,..." (4) Among the pre-1926 members only two (15%) served apprenticeships as a candidate or full member of the Politburo before being elevated to full voting status the first or second time. (5) Among the 12 who entered under Stalin during the 1926-38 period, ten (83%) had served such an apprenticeship.

With the possible exception of Gromyko (1973-), who long guided the vast Foreign Ministry, every other Politburo incumbent since 1926 has earned his spurs by successfully proving his leadership qualities in one or more of the labyrinths of the intertwined Soviet bureaucracies --i.e., the army, party, state and secret police hierarchies. Overwhelmingly, successful leadership at either, or both, the regional or republic Party level has been a key factor. Thus, some three-fourths of the incumbents since 1926 have had such experience as a vital part of their record of advancement.

Measurable differences between and among the 1926-38 Stalin Politburo, and the Lenin Politburo of 1917-21 and the transitional Stalin Politburo of 1922-25 provide the base for some interesting observations.

The score for the change-index for the years 1922-25 is a -13. Again, the index is a measure of stability and, as computed, the stronger the negative score the more stable the Politburo was in terms of turnover. Thus, there is empirical evidence to show that during that interregnum period, Stalin was biding his time. The changes came after

1925 and the change-index turns to a +4 for the 1926-38 period, largely reflecting the membership changes engineered by Stalin in 1926.

Already the mean age of the Politburo was increasing. Thus the mean age of the 1926-38 Politburo (47 years) was 21% greater than that of the 1917-21 Politburo (5). That process continued until the 1970s when actuarial reality came to be the major determinant of the age of the Politburo membership. In sum, given the nature of Kremlin politics, the Soviet Union was destined to reach, and has reached, a point of being ruled by a self-perpetuating gerontocracy. True, from time to time younger men (i.e., in their early 50s) are brought on board, but their induction has been the exception and never has had a significant impact on the aging process. As documented in our subsequent examination of what promises to be the beginning of a Gorbachev era, the fact that the mean age of the 1985 Politburo is a recent low of 66 years probably is an actuarial accident. Thus, our projection is that sometime in the 1990s, the mean age may even surpass the previous record of 70 years, reached in 1971.

There were no individuals of peasant origin on the Politburo between 1917 and 1925. The membership was dominated by men who came from intellectual and worker homes. Moreover, the majority was made up of individuals who had had at least some higher education. In sharp contrast the 1926-38 Politburo was dominated by men of village origin (63% peasant) and by men who had had no higher educational experience (85%).

Here, before proceeding, I must remind the reader again that at best numbers are but a pale reflection of the complexity of human reality. While I do believe that the method used to classify individuals as coming from worker, peasant or intellectual backgrounds has validity, often the situation was more complex than the numbers used would imply. For example, Khrushchev did come from a village; his father was of peasant origin. However, Khrushchev's father worked in the mines. Therefore, was Khrushchev of peasant orgin, worker origin, or both? Similarly, some of our calls as to whether the individual's educational experience was "higher" or "polytechnical" might be questioned. Here, our attempt was to distinguish between those whose training largely was confined to learning a trade (e.g., to be a railway engineer) as contrasted with those whose formal education involved historical and theoretical content --e.g., training as a mechanical engineer in contrast to learning how to operate machines.

Obviously, Politburo apprenticeship as a candidate or former member was not important prior to 1926. Since that time the Politburos have been dominated by people who have passed the test of close first-hand scrutiny, without the privilege of full power during their time of trial.

After 1926 Stalin was in his dominant position and his requirements for Politburo membership were significantly different from the requirements that had prevailed during the early years.

Political Truce During the War (1939-45)

The first law of politics for practicing politicians is that top priority always must be given to survival in office.

Of the eight members of the 1938 Politburo, the only Pole ever to serve as a full voting member of the Politburo, Kosior (1930-39), also had the honor of being the last Politburo member to be caught up in the Stalin purges of the 1930s and expelled. The remaining six were trusted Stalin lieutenants, and they were joined in 1939 by Nikita Khrushchev (1939-64) and Andrey Zhdanov (1939-48), a man considered to be Stalin's closest personal friend during his long years of rule. Thus, on the eve of World War II there were nine men at the Soviet helm, all of whom would remain in position for the next six years. Indeed, as shown in Profile 4, "The Stalin Politburo: 1939-45," the same held true for the four individuals who served as candidate members only during the period. None were removed from office while Stalin remained alive. Indeed, Andreev (1934-52) was the only member of the World War II leadership slated to be removed from office while Stalin continued to rule. Table 5 compares the demographic measures of the war-time Politburo with the measures for the pre-war Politburos.

Not surprisingly, the measures employed reveal that along with the interregnum period of 1922-25, the war-time Politburo was the most stable of all the Politburo periods. No one was removed as long as the war lasted.

For war-time leaders, they were quite young. The median age of the members for the whole period was 53. Ethnically, the Russian members accounted for two-thirds of the Politburo, plus the Georgian Stalin, Mikoyan, an Armenian, and Kaganovich, the only Jew to serve on the Politburo since the early years.

Table 5

COMPOSITE MEASURES OF MEANS OF POLITBURO PERIODS: 1917-45*

	1917-21	22-25	26-38	39-45
Number on Politburo	6	7	9	9
The change-index	+3	-13	+4	-13
% off from previous year (a)	3	4	10	2
% off health reasons (b)	0	4	2	0
% new (c)	4	8	14	3
Age Frst. Sec. first year	47	42	47	60
Politburo means				
Age	38	43	47	53
Total years served (d)	2	4	6	12
Origins in %				
Peasant	0	0	63	78
Worker	44	45	27	11
Intellectual	56	55	10	11
Russian	54	54	56	67
Ukrainian	0	0	2	0
Other Nationality	46	46	52	33
Education in %				
Some higher	80	69	15	0
Polytechnical	0	0	13	11
Experience in %				
Regional Frst. Sec.	12	7	10	33
Republic Frst. Sec.	0	0	17	11
Apprenticeship (e)	7	15	63	78
Secretariat or Orgburo	65	46	72	78
Presidium Sup. Sov.	41	31	70	66
Council of Ministers	58	62	74	89
Travel outside Bloc (f)	43	46	35	44

*Means for all of the years within each of the periods.

a-The percentage of the previous year's Politburo that is not returned, b-the percentage of the previous year's Politburo not returned for health reasons, c-the percentage of that year's Politburo that is new, d-years served at that point in time, e-previous service either as a candidate or full Politburo member, f-excluding travel prior to 1917.

Profile 4
THE STALIN POLITBURO, 1939-1945*

a Family Back.	b Nation-ality	Year into Party	c Higher Ed.	d Military Exp.	e Repub. or Region 1st Sec.	f Years Cand. Politburo or Presidium	f Years Full Politburo or Presidium
FULL VOTING MEMBERS							
STALIN, Iosif Vissarionovich, 1879-1953							
Wkr	Georg	1898	Theo	Genis	----	----	1917-1953
KALININ, Mikhail Ivanovich, 1875-1946							
Peas	Russ	1898	----	----	----	1919-1926?	1926-1946?
MOLOTOV, Vyaheslav Mikhaylovich, 1890-							
Peas	Russ	1906	Poly	----	----	1924?-1926	1926-1957
VOROSHILOV, Kliment Yefremovich, 1881-1969							
Peas	Russ	1903	----	Mshl	----	----	1926-1960
KAGANOVICH, Lazar Moissevich, 1893-							
Peas	Jewish	1911	----	Cmdr	Ukrain	1927-1930	1930-1957
ANDREEV, Andrei Andreevich, 1895-1971							
Peas	Russ	1914	----	----	----	1927-1934	1934-1952?
MIKOYAN, Ansastas Ivonovich, 1895-1978							
Peas	Arm	1915	Theo	----	Krai	1926-1935	1935-1966
KHRUSHCHEV, Nikita Sergeevich, 1894-1971							
Peas	Russ	1918	Poly	LtG	Oblast	1935-1939	1939-1964
ZHDANOV, Andrey Aleksandrovich, 1896-1948							
Int	Russ	1912?	----	Cmdr	Oblast	1935-1939	1939-1948
CANDIDATE MEMBERS ONLY DURING THE PERIOD							
BERIYA, Lavrentii Pavlovich, 1893-1953							
Peas	Georg	1917	Poly	Mshl	Georg	1939-1946	1946-1953
SHVERNIK, Nikolai Mikhailovich, 1888-1970							
Wkr?	Russ	1905	----	Cmdr	Oblast	1939-1952 1953-1957	1952-1953 1957-1964
KUZNETSOV, Vasilii Vasil'evich, 1901-							
Peas	Russ	1927	Eng	----	----	1944-1952 1977-	1952-1953

* The key to the profile categories, including an explanation of the abbreviations used, can be found on pages 9-12.

Sect. or Org.[g]	Pre-sidium Sup. Sov.[g]	Council of Ministers[g]	Other Important Experience	Travel Outside Bloc	Why Off Politb.	Cause of Death[h]
Fst	Yes	Pm	CmsNts	----	Died	Ntrl
----	Prs	----	----	----	Hlth	Ntrl
Yes	Yes	Pm	ForMin	Much	Expl	----
Yes	Prs	Yes	----	Some	Hlth	Ntrl
Yes	----	Yes	APG	----	Expl	----
Yes	Yes	Yes	Ag TU	----	Rem	Ntrl
----	Prs	Yes	----	Much	Hlth	Ntrl
Fst	----	Pm	----	Much	Hlth	Ntrl
Yes	----	Yes	----	----	Died	Ntrl
----	----	Yes	MVD Mshl	----	Expl	Exec
----	Prs	----	TU TU	Some Some	Rem Rem	---- Ntrl
Yes	Yes	----	Amb Dip TU	Much	Rem	----

Profile 4
THE STALIN POLITBURO, 1939-1945 (Continued)

a Family Back.	b Nation-ality	Year into Party	c Higher Ed.	d Military Exp.	e Repub. or Region 1st Sec.	Years Cand. (Politburo or Presidium)	Years Full (Politburo or Presidium)
SHCHERBAKOV, Aleksandr Sergeyevich, 1901-1945							
Wkr	Russ	1918	PolA	Cmdr	Oblast	1941-1945	----

g Sect. or Org.	g Pre- sidium Sup. Sov.	g Council of Ministers	Other Important Experience	Travel Outside Bloc	Why Off Politb.	h Cause of Death
----	----	Yes	Koms	----	Died	Ntrl

Compared to the earlier Politburos, the most striking difference in the 1939-45 body is that now men of peasant origin (78%) clearly dominated, and not one of the members had had any formal higher education. Understandably, with a war to pursue, all wore one or more second hats in key governmental posts. During their careers 89% also headed key ministeries and/or served on the Presidium of the Supreme Soviet.

Perhaps, the most important information to be gleaned from an analysis of demographic measures of the Soviet war-time leadership is that they did receive earthly rewards for their service. Among the eight, aside from Stalin, four were, or would become, the Soviet president or prime minister, including Khrushchev who was to become the first secretary. Among the six who are known to have died, their average lifespan was 74 years. Indeed, if Molotov and Kaganovich are still alive in 1986, both are in their mid-80s. Moreover, again aside from Stalin, their average tenure on the Politburo was 24 years.

Clearly, understandably, all domestic internal problems were placed on hold, including contests for power at the top. Stalin may have been a madman, but his madness did not extend to decimating the ranks of his closest supporters at the point in time when the Soviet system faced the gravest threat of all. The German invasion threatened not only the existence of the Soviet Union, but also the very lives of the members of the Politburo. Thus, what characterized Soviet politics between 1939 and 1945 more than anything else was a domestic political truce, especially within the Politburo.

Politburo politics were suspended for the duration of the war. Thus, perhaps the most important lesson to be learned from the demographics of that body during the period is that however ruthless and unbending Soviet leaders may be, when faced by a common threat of catastrophic proportions, they are capable of acting in unison for the common good.

Directing the Reconstruction (1946-51)

After the successful completion of the enormously costly war, Politburo politics returned to normal, although there was less-than-average turnover on that body until 1952.

Ironically, for the men in the Kremlin, victory in the war also meant the consumation of the Stalinist system. The fight against Hitler's army with the horrible loss of life had united the great mass of Soviet people into the system and behind the leaders in a way that nothing else could have done. Important pockets of dissent have emerged in the post-war years, but any serious base for mass resistance to the Kremlin's leadership has disappeared. As the late Merle Fainsod observed, in the early years mass terror was the "linchpin" that held the Stalinist system together. Now the "linchpin" was no longer needed. For whatever reasons, Stalin did not perceive the change, but Khrushchev did, and one of his most important acts was to remove terror as a key element of Soviet rule.

Another major fruit of the war was the addition of most of the previously independent states of Eastern Europe to the empire. Thus, the iron curtain was moved west and then Stalin welded it shut as tightly as ever.

Domestically, all effort was concentrated upon rebuilding the war-ravaged economy. All priority to the construction of heavy industry was the "first commandment." As Khrushchev records, not only was agriculture ignored, but Stalin stood idly by and did nothing when famine struck the Ukraine in 1946-47. The charlatan scientist Lysenko ruled agricultural science with Stalin's blessing.

Still, from 1945 through 1951 there was relative calm in the Kremlin. No new major purge was initiated. Kalinin (1926-46) died in 1946 and Zhdanov (1939-48) died in 1948, both probably of natural causes. As long as Stalin remained relatively healthy, only the tragic ending to the brilliant director of Gosplan, Voznesenskiy (1947-49), marred the scene. He was expelled and executed for treason in 1950.

During Stalin's 30 years of rule, this period had the second lowest explusion rate for Politburo members. Thus, of the 20 men who served under Stalin in the pre-war period (1922-39) nine (46%) were expelled, while in the 1946-51 period only 8% were expelled --i.e. only Voznesenskiy among the 13 who served during these years. There were no expulsions during the 1939-45 period. Further, as shown in Profile 5, "The Stalin Politburo: 1946-51," the two individuals who served as candidate members only during the period were retained by Stalin through 1951.

Excluding the extraordinary year 1952, Table 6 summarizes the demographic changes that occurred in the Poltiburo during the sub-periods identified here.

Profile 5
THE STALIN POLITBURO, 1946-51*

a Family Back.	b Nation- ality	Year into Party	c Higher Ed.	d Military Exp.	e Repub. or Region 1st Sec	f Years Cand. Politburo or Presidium	f Years Full
FULL VOTING MEMBERS							
STALIN, Iosif Vissarionovich, 1879-1953							
Wkr	Georg	1898	Theo	Genis	----	----	1917-1953
MOLOTOV, Vyacheslav Mikhaylovich, 1890-							
Peas	Russ	1906	Poly	----	----	1924?-1926	1926-1957
VOROSHILOV, Kliment Yefremovich, 1881-1969							
Peas	Russ	1903	----	Mshl	----	----	1926-1960
KAGANOVICH, Lazar Moissevich, 1893-							
Peas	Jewish	1911	----	Cmdr	Ukrain	1927-1930	1930-1957
ANDREEV, Andrei Andreevich, 1895-1971							
Peas	Russ	1914	----	----	----	1927-1934	1934-1952?
MIKOYAN, Ansastas Ivonovich, 1895-1978							
Peas	Arm	1915	Theo	----	Krai	1926-1935	1935-1966
KHRUSHCHEV, Nikita Sergeevich, 1894-1971							
Peas	Russ	1918	Poly	LtG	Oblast	1935-1939	1939-1964
ZHDANOV, Andrey Aleksandrovich, 1896-1948							
Int	Russ	1912?	----	Cmdr	Oblast	1935-1939	1939-1948
BERIYA, Lavrentii Pavlovich, 1896-1953							
Peas	Georg	1917	Poly	Mshl	Georg	1939-1946	1946-1953
MALENKOV,Georgii Maksimilianovich, 1902-							
Wkr?	Russ	1920	----	Cmdr	----	1941-1946	1946-1957
VOZNESENSKIY, Nikolay Alekseyevich, 1903-1950							
Int	Russ	B1924	PolyA	----	----	1941-1947	1947-1949
BULGANIN, Nikolai Aleksandrovich, 1895-1975							
Wkr?	Russ	1917	----	Mshl	----	1946-1948	1948-1958
KOSYGIN, Aleksey Nikolaevich, 1904-1980							
Wkr?	Russ	1927	Poly	----	----	1946-1948 1957-1960	1948-1952 1960-1980

* The key to the profile categories, including an explanation of the abbreviations used, can be found on pages 9-12.

Sect. or Org.[g]	Presidium Sup. Sov.[g]	Council of Ministers[g]	Other Important Experience	Travel Outside Bloc	Why Off Politb.	Cause of Death[h]
Fst	Yes	Pm	CmsNts	----	Died	Ntrl
Yes	Yes	Pm	ForMin	Much	Expl	----
Yes	Prs	Yes	----	Some	Hlth	Ntrl
Yes	----	Yes	APG	----	Expl	----
Yes	Yes	Yes	Ag TU	----	Rem	Ntrl
----	Prs	Yes	----	Much	Hlth	Ntrl
Fst	----	Pm	----	Much	Hlth	Ntrl
Yes	----	Yes	----	----	Died	Ntrl
----	----	Yes	MVD Mshl	----	Expl	Exec
Fst	----	Pm	APG	Some	Expl	----
----	----	Yes	Gos	----	Expl	Exec
----	----	Pm	APG	Much	Expl	Ntrl
----	----	Yes Pm	Gos	Much Much	Rem Hlth	---- Ntrl

Profile 5
THE STALIN POLITBURO, 1946-1951 (Continued)

a Family Back.	b Nation-ality	Year into Party	c Higher Ed.	d Military Exp.	e Repub. or Region 1st Sec.	f Years Cand. Politburo or Presidium	f Years Full Politburo or Presidium
CANDIDATE MEMBERS ONLY DURING THE PERIOD							
SHVERNIK, Nikolai Mikhailovich, 1888-1970							
Wkr?	Russ	1905	----	Cmdr	Oblast	1939-1952 1953-1957	1952-1953 1957-1964
KUZNETSOV, Vasilii Vasil'evich, 1901-							
Peas	Russ	1927	Eng	----	----	1944-1952 1977-	1952-1953

g Sect. or Org.	g Pre- sidium Sup. Sov.	g Council of Ministers	Other Important Experience	Travel Outside Bloc	Why Off Politb.	h Cause of Death
----	Prs	----	TU TU	Some Some	Rem Rem	---- Ntrl
Yes	Yes	----	Amb Dip TU	Much	Rem	----

Table 6

COMPOSITE MEASURES OF MEANS OF POLITBURO PERIODS: 1917-51*

	1917-21	22-25	26-38	39-45	46-51
Number on Politburo	6	7	9	9	11
The change-index	+3	-13	+4	-13	-8
% off from previous year (a)	3	4	10	2	3
% off health reasons (b)	0	4	2	0	3
% new (c)	4	8	14	3	8
Age Frst. Sec. first year	47	42	47	60	67
Politburo means					
Age	38	43	47	53	55
Total years served (d)	2	4	6	12	13
Origins in %					
Peasant	0	0	63	78	64
Worker	44	45	27	11	30
Intellectual	56	55	10	11	6
Russian	54	54	56	67	64
Ukrainian	0	0	2	0	0
Other Nationality	46	46	52	33	36
Education in %					
Some higher	80	69	15	0	3
Polytechnical	0	0	13	11	33
Experience in %					
Regional Frst. Sec.	12	7	10	33	23
Republic Frst. Sec.	0	0	17	11	17
Apprenticeship (e)	7	15	63	78	82
Secretariat or Orgburo	65	46	72	78	67
Presidium Sup. Sov.	41	31	70	66	46
Council of Ministers	58	62	74	89	100
Travel outside Bloc (f)	43	46	35	44	57

*Means for all of the years within each of the periods.

a-The percentage of the previous year's Politburo that is not returned, b-the percentage of the previous year's Politburo not returned for health reasons, c-the percentage of that year's Politburo that is new, d-years served at that point in time, e-previous service either as a candidate or full Politburo member, f-excluding travel prior to 1917.

The Extraordinary Class of 1952

One of the least momentous changes that occurred in the extraordinary year of 1952 was that the Politburo name was dropped and, until 1966 when the name was restored, the body was called the Presidium of the Central Committee of the CPSU. However, to minimize confusion between that body and the Presidium of the Supreme Soviet, I have consistently used the term Politburo in this study.

One year does not normally constitute a period of history, but the events of 1952 are so extraordinary and so important to understanding Politburo politics that what occurred during Stalin's final months deserves special attention. Simply stated, although Stalin had been able to contain his madness earlier, indeed use it to his advantage, towards the end, his paranoia overwhelmed him. He became persuaded that the doctors who treated him were, in fact, attempting to poison him. Of course, the doctors were arrested. Further, surely he believed that some of his Politburo colleagues were plotting against him.

Again the change-index for the 1946-51 period is negative. That fact will further support the contention that after the 1926 shakeup Stalin had his men in place. They had served him well during the war and they were the men he wanted to build the peace.

Stalin himself was by then an old man (67 in 1946), but the Politburo as a whole was still relatively young and vigorous. Two-thirds were of peasant origin and nearly one-third came from worker homes.

Still, the USSR was ruled by men who had had no formal higher education, although those with polytechnical training were coming to the fore (33%).

Not surprisingly, given the reemphasis on industrial construction, 100% of the 1946-51 body held, or were to hold, ministerial posts.

In his memoirs Khrushchev contends that the 16 members added to the Politburo in 1952, many of whom were quite obscure on the Soviet scene (see below), were brought on board by a sick and befuddled Stalin who wanted to secure the votes to purge the Politburo of members he regarded as undesirable. (6) The demography of the extraordinary class of 1952 supports Khrushchev's contention. Indeed, the biggest holes that exist in the biographic data are concentrated on the 1952 Politburo. Thus, for three of the members I have no information on the date they entered the CPSU or whether or not they had any military experience.

Had Stalin lived another year or more, undoubtedly he would have been able to repeat his 1926 maneuver. The newcomers would have provided the support needed to oust the older unwanted incumbents. Again he would have been surrounded by a group of relatively young sycophants, who would have done his every bidding. The average age of the new entries was only 53, in contrast to that of the incumbents, excluding Stalin (73), which was 59.

Table 7 reveals the remarkable differences between the swollen class of 1952 and the earlier pre-war Politburos.

Profile 6, "The Stalin Politburo: 1952," shows that Stalin was not content with just stuffing the full-voting Politburo. In addition to the 16 new voting members, he brought on board six, relatively young, non-voting members, including Leonid Brezhnev (1957-82) who was only 46 in 1952.

The magnitude of the change wrought by Stalin is shown in the change-index which jumped to a +66, largely reflecting the fact that 64% of the 1952 Poliburo were newcomers.

There was also a radical change in the makeup of the body in terms of family origin, which reversed the peasant-worker ratio. Now those who came from worker families were nearly twice those who were peasant origin.

Most interestingly, the bulk of the 1952 inductees had had at least some higher education. However, they were almost wholly without high-level experience on three scores: they had not served an apprenticeship as candidate Politburo members; they had not held top Moscow administrative posts; they had not distinguished themselves as successful first secretaries of republic or regional organs. In sum, they were drawn from the bottom rung of the second level of Soviet officialdom and not from the top of that group from which normally new Politburo members are drawn.

Beyond their lack of top level administrative experience another factor may distinguish the 16 1952 inductees. Of the 13 for which there is such data, 69% had had military experience, either holding high military commissions or having seen active service in the Civil War or World War II.

Table 7

COMPOSITE MEASURES OF MEANS OF POLITBURO PERIODS: 1917-52*

	1917-21	22-25	26-38	39-45	46-51	52
Number on Politburo	6	7	9	9	11	25
The change-index	+3	-13	+4	-13	-8	+66
% off from						
previous year (a)	3	4	10	2	3	18
% off health reasons (b)	0	4	2	0	3	0
% new (c)	4	8	14	3	8	64
Age Frst. Sec. first year	47	42	47	60	67	74
Politburo means						
Age	38	43	47	53	55	56
Total years served (d)	2	4	6	12	13	6
Origins in %						
Peasant	0	0	63	78	64	36
Worker	44	45	27	11	30	60
Intellectual	56	55	10	11	6	4
Russian	54	54	56	67	64	72
Ukrainian	0	0	2	0	0	0
Other Nationality	46	46	52	33	36	38
Education in %						
Some higher	80	69	15	0	3	36
Polytechnical	0	0	13	11	33	28
Experience in %						
Regional Frst. Sec.	12	7	10	33	23	16
Republic Frst. Sec.	0	0	17	11	17	4
Apprenticeship (e)	7	15	63	78	82	36
Secretariat or Orgburo	65	46	72	78	67	56
Presidium Sup. Sov.	41	31	70	66	46	40
Council of Ministers	58	62	74	89	100	56
Travel outside Bloc (f)	43	46	35	44	57	60

*Means for all of the years within each of the periods.

a-The percentage of the previous year's Politburo that is not returned, b-the percentage of the previous year's Politburo not returned for health reasons, c-the percentage of that year's Politburo that is new, d-years served at that point in time, e-previous service either as a candidate or full Politburo member, f-excluding travel prior to 1917.

Profile 6
THE STALIN POLITBURO, 1952*

a Family Back.	b Nation-ality	Year into Party	c Higher Ed.	d Military Exp.	e Repub. or Region 1st Sec.	f Years Cand. Politburo or Presidium	f Years Full Politburo or Presidium
FULL VOTING MEMBERS							
STALIN, Iosif Vissarionovich, 1879-1953							
Wkr	Georg	1898	Theo	Genis	----	----	1917-1953
MOLOTOV, Vyacheslav Mikhaylovich, 1890-							
Peas	Russ	1906	Poly	----	----	1924?-1926	1926-1957
VOROSHILOV, Kliment Yefremovich, 1881-1969							
Peas	Russ	1903	----	Mshl	----	----	1926-1960
KAGANOVICH, Lazar Moissevich, 1893-							
Peas	Jewish	1911	----	Cmdr	Ukrain	1927-1930	1930-1957
MIKOYAN, Ansastas Ivonovich, 1895-1978							
Peas	Arm	1915	Theo	----	Krai	1926-1935	1935-1966
KHRUSHCHEV, Nikita Sergeevich, 1894-1971							
Peas	Russ	1918	Poly	LtG	Oblast	1935-1939	1939-1964
BERIYA, Lavrentii Pavlovich, 1893-1953							
Peas	Georg	1917	Poly	Mshl	Georg	1939-1946	1946-1953
MALENKOV, Georgii Maksimilianovich, 1902-							
Wkr?	Russ	1920	----	Cmdr	----	1941-1946	1946-1957
BULGANIN, Nikolai Aleksandrovich, 1895-1975							
Wkr?	Russ	1917	----	Mshl	----	1946-1948	1948-1958
ANDRIANOV, Vasilii Mikhailovich, 1902-							
Wkr?	Russ	Nd	Nd	Nd	Gorod	----	1952-1953
ARISTOV, Averkii Borisovich, 1903-1973							
Wkr?	Russ	1921	Poly	----	Oblast	----	1952-1953 1957-1961
CHESNOKOV, Dmitrii Ivanovich, 1910-1973							
Wkr?	Russ	Nd	Univ?	Nd	Krai	----	1952-1953
IGNAT'YEV, Semen Denisovich, 1904-							
Wkr?	Tatar?	Nd	Nd	Nd	Oblast	----	1952-1953

* The key to the profile categories, including an explanation of the abbreviations used, can be found on pages 9-12.

g Sect. or Org.	g Pre-sidium Sup. Sov.	g Council of Ministers	Other Important Experience	Travel Outside Bloc	Why Off Politb.	h Cause of Death
Fst	Yes	Pm	CmsNts	----	Died	Ntrl
Yes	Yes	Pm	ForMin	Much	Expl	----
Yes	Prs	Yes	----	Some	Hlth	Ntrl
Yes	----	Yes	APG	----	Expl	----
----	Prs	Yes	----	Much	Hlth	Ntrl
Fst	----	Pm	----	Much	Hlth	Ntrl
----	----	Yes	MVD Mshl	----	Expl	Exec
Fst	----	Pm	APG	Some	Expl	----
----	----	Pm	APG	Much	Expl	Ntrl
----	----	----	FstSec Len	----	Rem	----
Yes	----	----	Koms TU	----	Rem	----
			Amb	Some	Rem	Ntrl
----	----	----	EdKom Prof	----	Rem	Ntrl
Yes	Yes	----	MVD	----	Hlth	----

Profile 6
THE STALIN POLITBURO, 1952 (Continued)

a Family Back.	b Nation- ality	Year into Party	c Higher Ed.	d Military Exp.	e Repub. or Region 1st Sec	f Years Cand. Politburo or Presidium	f Years Full Politburo or Presidium
FULL VOTING MEMBERS							
KOROTCHENKO, Dem'yan Sergeevich, 1894-1969							
Peas	Ukrain	1918	PolA	Cmdr	----	1957-1961	1952-1953
KUUSINEN, Otto Vil'gel'movich, 1881-1964							
Wkr?	Fin	1904	Univ	Cmdr	----	----	1952-1953 1957-1964
KUZNETSOV, Vasilii Vasil'evich, 1901-							
Peas	Russ	1927	Eng	----	----	1944-1952 1977-	1952-1953
MALYSHEV, Vyacheslav Aleksandrovich, 1902-1957							
Int	Russ	1926	Poly	CIG	----	----	1952-1953
MEL'NIKOV, Leonid Georievich, 1906-1981							
Wkr?	Russ	1928	Poly	----	Ukrain	1953-1956	1952-1953
MIKHAILOV, Nikolai Aleksandrovich, 1906-1982							
Wkr?	Russ	1930	Univ?	----	----	----	1952-1953
PERVUKHIN, Mikhail Georgievich, 1904-1978							
Wkr?	Russ	1919	Eng	LtG	----	1957-1961	1952-1957
PONOMARENKO, Panteleimon Kondrat'evich, 1902-							
Wkr?	Russ	1925	Eng	Cmdr	Kazaak	1953-1956	1952-1953
SABUROV, Maksim Zakharovich, 1900-							
Wkr?	Russ	1920	Inst	Cmdr	----	----	1952-1957
SHKIRYATOV, Matevi Mikhailovich, 1883-1954							
Wkr?	Russ	1906	----	Cmdr	----	----	1952-1953
SHVERNIK, Nikolai Mikhailovich, 1888-1970							
Wkr?	Russ	1905	----	Cmdr	Oblast	1939-1952 1953-1957	1952-1953 1957-1964
SUSLOV, Mikhail Andreevich, 1902-1982							
Peas	Russ	1921	Ecn	Cmdr	Oblast	----	1952-1953 1955-1982

Sect. or Org. [g]	Pre-sidium Sup. Sov. [g]	Council of Ministers [g]	Other Important Experience	Travel Outside Bloc	Why Off Polit.	Cause of Death [h]
----	Yes	----	----	----	Rem	Ntrl
----	Yes	----	Prs KarFin	Some	Rem	----
Yes				Some	Died	Ntrl
Yes	Yes	----	Amb Dip TU	Much	Rem	----
----	----	Yes	----	----	Rem	Ntrl
----	----	Yes	----	----	Rem	Ntrl
Yes	----	----	AgP Koms Amb	Some	Rem	Ntrl
----	----	Yes	Amb Koms	Some	Rem	Ntrl
Yes	----	Yes	Amb Dip	Much	Rem	----
----	----	Yes	Gos Koms	Much	Rem	----
----	----	----	----	----	Rem	Ntrl
----	Prs	----	TU	Some	Rem	----
			TU	Some	Rem	Ntrl
Yes	Yes	----	AgP	----	Rem	----
Yes				Much	Died	Ntrl

Profile 6
THE STALIN POLITBURO, 1952 (Continued)

a Family Back.	b Nation- ality	Year into Party	c Higher Ed.	d Military Exp.	e Repub. or Region 1st Sec	f Years Cand. Politburo or Presidium	f Years Full Politburo or Presidium
CANDIDATE MEMBERS ONLY DURING THE YEAR							
BREZHNEV, Leonid Il'ich, 1906-1982							
Wkr?	Russ	1931	Eng	LtG	Kazak	1952-1953 1956-1957	1957-1982
IGNATOV, Nikolai Grigor'evich, 1901-1966							
Peas	Russ	1924	PolA	----	Oblast	1952-1953	1957-1961
PATOLICHEV, Nikolai Semenovich, 1908-							
Peas	Russ	1931	Poly	----	Bel	1952-1953	----
TEVOSYAN, Ivan Fredorovich, 1902-1958							
Wkr	Azeri	1919	Poly	Cmdr	----	1952-1953	----
VYSHINSKY, Andrei Yanuar'evich, 1883-1954							
Wkr?	Russ	1903	Lw	Cmdr	----	1952-1953	----
ZVEREV, Arsenii Grigor'evich, 1900-1969							
Peas	Russ	1919	Ecn	Cmdr	----	1952-1953	----

Sect. or Org.[g]	Presidium Sup. Sov.[g]	Council of Ministers[g]	Other Important Experience	Travel Outside Bloc	Why Off Politb.	Cause of Death[h]
Fst	Prs	Yes	----	Much	Died	Ntrl
Yes	----	Yes	----	----	Rem	Ntrl
----	Yes	----	Dip	Much	Rem	----
----	----	Yes	Amb	Some	Rem	Ntrl
----	----	Yes	ForMin Prof	Much	Expl	Ntrl
----	----	Yes	Prof	----	Rem	Ntrl

Of course, Stalin's plans were not realized because he died in 1953. Although four of the 15 members ousted in 1953 (Beriya, plus 14 of the class of 1952) were to be returned later for a longer tenure on the Politburo, that body was reduced to a more nearly normal size.

NOTES

1. The same analysis suggests that at that time age was not a factor influencing the length of survival.

2. Although there are important holes in our knowledge about the 1922 Politburo, our conjecture is that Tomsky was a Lenin man because he entered the Politburo in 1922 --the 11th Congress held that year was in March, but Lenin's serious illness did not strike him until May. Also Tomsky was a strong supporter of Lenin's NEP, which may well have been key to his appointment.

3. For a thoughtful discussion of the differences between "inner-directed" and "other-directed" individuals, see David Riesman, Nathan Glazier and Raul Denney THE LONELY CROWD, Garden City, Doubleday Anchor Books, 1953, especially p. 32 ff.

4. Seweryn Bialer, STALIN'S SUCCESSORS: LEADERSHIP STABILITY AND CHANGE IN THE SOVIET UNION, New York: Cambridge University Press, 1980, p. 72.

5. As we shall see, several of the individuals inducted as full members in 1952 were removed the next year. However, that brief service did serve as a kind of apprenticeship and, subsequently, Khrushchev returned them to the Politburo as full members for longer periods of service.

6. KHRUSHCHEV REMEMBERS (Trans. and Ed. by Strobe Talbott, Int. and Commentary by Edward Crankshaw), Boston: Little, Brown and Company, 1970, pp. 276-287.

PART THREE

A New Deal in Soviet Politics

Although essential features of the political house that Stalin built remain in place, not only is mass terror gone, along with the practice of imprisoning and executing failed Politburo members, but other important changes have been made as well. Therefore, without ignoring what can be learned from the Lenin-Stalin experience, one must draw from post-1952 patterns the major guide to understanding the present, or forecasting the future of Politburo affairs.

An examination of "The Khrushchev Legacy" (below) reveals that most of the changes that occurred between 1953 and 1986 occurred during Khrushchev's leadership.

Just as the survival of an individual is very much dependent upon that individual's ability to adapt to changing circumstances, so are political systems dependent upon an ability to adapt to change. Thus, another key focus in what follows is an attempt to perceive what have been, and are, the major demands imposed on the post-1953 Politburos, how the leaders have viewed the demands, and what they have tried to do about them.

When faced with changing demands which pose a threat to continuing in office, presidents, prime ministers, and Soviet first secretaries of the CPSU often look first to possible shifts in their cabinets. Perhaps there are Politburo incumbents resisting needed changes? Always there are eager candidates for high office waiting in the wings, individuals apt to support policy initiatives by the first secretary.

That shifts in the makeup of cabinets occur at the time of leadership succession is part of the historical record. Also, important changes in leadership personnel often occur within an administration. As shown above, such changes repeatedly occurred in the Soviet Politburo during the 30 years of Stalin's rule. How about the post-1952 period? Should the Khrushchev and Brezhnev eras be viewed as single periods of time, or were there sub-periods within each of those eras?

One important reason for dividing both the Khrushchev and Brezhnev eras into sub-periods is the historical record of important policy changes within each of the eras. That such periods exist is supported by the discovery that significant shifts in Politburo personnel far above the norm occurred in both 1957 and 1971, years identified as marking the beginning of identifiable sub-periods within the Khrushchev and Brezhnev eras.

Not surprisingly, the 1957 challenge to Khrushchev's leadership resulted in a major shift in Politburo membership. Thus, the division of the Khrushchev era into two leadership periods, 1953-57 and 1958-63, seems quite obvious.

As discussed below (see "The Brezhnev Era"), the division of the Brezhnev era into two leadership periods, 1964-72 and 1973-81, is not so obvious. Still, important policy shifts did occur early in the 1970s, and there were important changes in the Politburo membership in 1973.

The personnel change-index reveals that there were an unusual number of changes in the makeup of the Politburo in each of the years identified as marking the beginning of a new period --i.e., 1953, 1957, 1964, 1973, 1982 and 1985.

The personnel change-index recorded in Table 8 is accompanied by other measures of Politburo demographic change in the years identified as the beginning of sub-periods since 1952.

Table 8

MEASURES OF POLITBURO CHANGES: FIRST YEAR OF PERIODS

	1953	1957	1964	1973	1982	1985
Number on Politburo	9	16	11	16	11	13
The change-index	+40	+101	+20	+20	+11	+20
% off from previous year (a)	64	55	25	15	29	18
% off health reasons (b)	8	0	8	0	14	9
% new that year (c)	0	63	18	19	9	23
Age Frst. Sec.	59	63	58	67	68	54
Politburo means						
Age that year	58	58	59	63	67	66
Total years served (d)	14	5	6	7	7	6
Origins in %						
Peasant	56	56	45	38	36	23
Worker	44	44	55	56	45	62
Intellectual	0	0	0	6	9	15
Russian	78	75	64	56	64	62
Ukrainian	0	6	27	25	18	15
Other Nationality	22	19	9	19	18	23
Education in %						
Some higher	22	50	36	40	64	54
Polytechnical	22	19	45	50	36	46
Experience in %						
Regional Frst. Sec.	22	56	73	31	36	54
Republic Frst. Sec.	11	19	18	38	18	15
Apprenticeship (e)	78	88	91	69	91	77
Secretariat	56	75	55	44	45	31
Presidium Sup. Sov.	33	31	27	38	50	23
Council of Ministers	100	56	55	56	43	46
Travel outside Bloc (f)	89	75	91	88	100	92

a-The percentage of the previous year's Politburo that is not returned, b-the percentage of the previous year's Politburo not returned for health reasons, c-the percentage of that year's Politburo that is new, d-years served at that point in time, e-previous service either as a candidate or full Politburo member, f-excluding travel prior to 1917.

5

The Khrushchev Era (1953–63)

There was a mini-interregnum between the end of the Stalin era and the beginning of the Khrushchev era.

On March 5, 1953, Stalin died. On March 7, 1953, a plenary session of the CC CPSU reduced the Politburo to 10 members with Malenkov's name at the head of the list. However, 7 days later (March 14) the plenary session removed Malenkov (1946-57) from the Secretariat, and the published list of the members of that body had Khrushchev's name first. Finally, by September of that year, things were fully sorted out. Thus, at a September 1953 plenary session of the CC CPSU Khrushchev was "elected" to the position of first secretary.

One of the most revealing insights gained from the analysis reported here is recognition of how significant, indeed, profound, were the changes that occurred during Khrushchev's decade in power. One must conclude that Khrushchev's impact was such that he left the Soviet Prometheus at least partially unbound. Some of the Stalin shackles remain, but not all.

Who in 1952 foresaw that Stalin's successor would deliver a stinging indictment of some of Stalin's major crimes? Khrushchev did not totally end the incarceration of political prisoners, but under his rule millions were released from prison and rehabilitated. Further, posthumously, the names of many, but not all, of the Soviet citizens who had been executed or who died in prison were restored to places of honor.

Who would have predicted before their release that Dudintsev's NOT BY BREAD ALONE and Solzhenitsyn's ONE DAY IN THE LIFE OF IVAN DENISOVICH would be published in the Soviet Union? For many, an even more profound publishing event was the 1956 appearance of the first statistical handbook published in the USSR in decades. Then and now there are many important omissions in the annual NARODNOE KHOZYAISTVO (PEOPLE'S ECONOMY) volumes, but at their worst they are a 1,000% improvement over what was available before.

Without precedent, Khrushchev was a Soviet leader who smiled, joked, laughed and sometimes cursed in public. Also, without precedent, he traveled abroad, pounded his shoe on a table in the UN, showed genuine concern for the citizens' welfare and, however unsuccessful, focused major concern on the serious problems of Soviet agriculture.

As documented in the Epigraph to this volume, Khrushchev believed that the top leaders must both "understand everything" and be "responsible for everything." Yet, in stark contrast to those of Stalin, Khrushchev's pronouncements were not always holy writ proclaimed from remote, unchallengeable Olympian heights. He was human, and capable of admitting something previously unthinkable: that the first secretary of the CPSU might even be wrong!

To this writer, much that was the essence of Khrushchev and his leadership style is revealed in a passage of a speech he gave in Kiev. The President of the Ukraine Academy of Agricultural Science had had the audacity to suggest that past errors had been rooted in faulty Party instructions. Here is Khrushchev's response, an almost poignant plea:

> Comrade Vlasyuk's statement (that the Party was at fault) shows his lack of principle. Comrade Vlasyuk, you will now cite my words and say: "Comrade Khrushchev said thus and so." Am I the highest authority in agricultural Science? You are the President of the Ukraine Republic Academy of Agricultural Sciences and I am the Secretary of the Party Central Committee. You must help me in these matters, and not I you. (Applause) I might be wrong, and if I am, you, as an honest scientist, should say: "Comrade Khrushchev, you do not quite understand this matter." If you explain things to me correctly, I will thank you for it. Let us say that I was wrong. But you will say, "Comrade Khrushchev said this and I supported him...." (1)

For the great masses of the Soviet Union, Nikita Khrushchev was the first flesh-and-blood human being to serve as their leader. Like the Tsars, Lenin and emphatically Stalin were remote untouchable "little fathers." Of course, if the "little father" knew what was going wrong in the village he would fix it, but he did not know and was too busy doing other more important things.

In his ten years at the top, Nikita Khrushchev saw more of the Soviet Union and met and talked to more of its citizens than any Soviet leader before or since.

Finally, in this introduction to the Khrushchev era, was it just a coincidence that Khrushchev was the first and only first secretary to have a woman on his Politburo, Ekaterina Furtseva (1957-61), who also was the Minister of Culture? I think not. Khrushchev too came from the same mold that has cast those who have made it to the top of Soviet political leadership. Yet, there were some special qualities in his makeup which mark him as an unique Soviet leader. Modern societies elsewhere in the world have come to realize that leadership talents are not a male monopoly, but not the Soviet Union.

As discussed in the closing sections of this work, the future health of the USSR, perhaps even the survival of the system, requires important reforms, including some in the leadership realm. As in all states, top quality leadership is not an overly abundant commodity in the USSR. To largely ignore, as the USSR does, the leadership talents of its women is a serious oversight. Thus, if one is searching for indicators of the future health of the USSR, I submit that a major indicator that needs tracking is the changing role, if any, of women in top Soviet leadership positions.

Khrushchev Attacks the Agricultural Problem (1953-56)

Solving the agricultural problem was Khrushchev's overwhelming domestic concern.

Not only did he repeatedly visit the farms and villages, but he made three profound changes in Soviet agriculture. He presided over the plowing up of a vast area of some 40 million hectares of virgin lands in the so-called "new lands region" of Kazakhstan and adjacent regions of the Southern RSFSR. He inaugurated the amalgamation campaign which was to increase enormously the average farm size and, thus, allow the Party fully to penetrate the kolkhozy and sovkhozy. Further, when the Party had captured the farms, in 1958 he abandoned the Machine-Tractor Stations, as they were no longer needed to maintain control over the farms.

His major agricultural reforms will be discussed in more detail later, but because the new lands venture came in Khrushchev's early years, and because it figured in both his successes and failures as a leader, some essential points need to be made about the new lands at this juncture.

Adding the new lands to the Soviet grain growing area shifted the center of Soviet grain production hundreds of kilometers to the east. However, farming in the new lands area is much more of a gamble than it is in the more established grain regions. Often a good grain growing year in the Ukraine is a poor one in Kazakhstan. Yet, that very fact has served as a plus. There is no doubt that Soviet grain production would have been far lower than it has been in recent decades without the new lands contribution. Yet, there have been serious prices to pay.

Some will argue, with considerable truth on their side, that the long-run solution to the Soviet grain problem lies in investment in the more reliable grain growing areas, accompanied by significant changes in the organization and management of the farms. Be this as it may, the Soviet leadership has viewed the new lands venture as a major success, especially in the early years.

In 1956 the USSR produced a bumper crop. Production in 1958 was even better, when weather conditions surely were the best they had been since the turn of the century. Ebulliently, Khrushchev proclaimed that the Soviet grain problem had been solved, that within a few short years the USSR would surpass US agricultural production and, subsequently, for the first time, a detailed statistical handbook on agriculture was published in 1960.

During the period 1953-56 ten incumbents served under Khrushchev. In 1953 Khrushchev was 59, by 1957 he would be 64. The average age of the members of the Politburo during the period was 59. Their family origins were 60% peasant and 40% worker. The nationality composition was 75% Russian, while the other 25% constituted one Jew, one Armenian and one Ukrainian, although all did not serve the full period. In the education realm 29% had had at least some higher education, while 16% had had polytechnical training. Indeed, among the 12 individuals who served under him during the period as candidate members only, 58% had had at least some higher education. See Profile 7, "The Khrushchev Politburo: 1953-56."

As far as previous experience is concerned, 40% had served, or were serving, as regional or republic Party first secretaries. When service as a candidate member of the Politburo is combined with having been a full member on the 1952-53 Politburo, 80% had had such an apprenticeship. Prior to, or during their time in office, 85% traveled outside of the Bloc.

At that time the average length of service on the Politburo was 14 years. No one was expelled or removed from the Politburo. Thus, the change-index for the years 1953-56 was a +2, slightly above neutral.

Khrushchev Repeats the Pattern (1957-63)

The demographic changes of the Politburo that occurred during the Khrushchev era, especially the wholesale turnover of membership in 1957, strongly support a conclusion that Khrushchev had taken to heart the lessons learned during Stalin's rule. Again, to set the stage for the events of 1957, all but two of the extraordinary class of 1952 were removed in 1953. Stalin, of course, died. Beriya (1946-53) was executed in 1953, and Malenkov (1946-57) effectively was neutered by his removal from the post of first secretary after only a few days in that office.

If Politburo minutes have been kept, perhaps at some future time what really happened in the Kremlin in 1957 will be released. Unfortunately, my reexamination of what is known in light of the demographics may serve only to confuse the record at this time.

As this writer sees it, the key issue is when were the crucial votes taken in 1957, and who were the full voting members of the Politburo at those times? In addition to the meetings of the Politburo, four Central Committee plenums were held in 1957: one in February, one in June, one in October and one in December. No changes in the makeup of the Politburo occurred in February, although Kozlov (1957-64) was made a candidate member at that time. Late that spring Khrushchev and Bulganin (1948-58) traveled to Finland, and we are told that upon their return Khrushchev was informed that he had been voted out of office by the colleagues who remained in Moscow. If this is correct, then I submit that a key question arises over who voted which way in the in-house deliberations prior to the quite extraordinary Plenum which met June 29th.

Michael Kort reports that the vote was taken June 19th and a seven-to-four majority against Khrushchev included Voroshilov (1926-60). (2) Alec Nove also reports a vote of seven-to-four against Khrushchev. (3) The Medvedevs claim the vote was eight-to-four, the four supporters of Khrushchev being Suslov (1955-82), Furtseva (1957-82), Mikoyan (1935-88) and, of course, Khrushchev himself. (4) Yet, my reading of the record is that the induction of Furtseva, Brezhnev and the other members of the class of 1957 did not occur until the June 29th meeting of the Plenum. Further, why was Voroshilov not expelled as a member of the "anti-Party group?"

Profile 7
THE KHRUSHCHEV POLITBURO, 1953-1956*

a Family Back.	b Nation- ality	Year into Party	c Higher Ed.	d Military Exp.	e Repub. or Region 1st Sec	f Years Cand. Politburo or Presidium	f Years Full Politburo or Presidium
FULL VOTING MEMBERS							
MOLOTOV, Vyacheslav Mikhaylovich, 1890-							
Peas	Russ	1906	Poly	----	----	1924?-1926	1926-1957
VOROSHILOV, Kliment Yefremovich, 1881-1969							
Peas	Russ	1903	----	Mshl	----	----	1926-1960
KAGANOVICH, Lazar Moissevich, 1893-							
Peas	Jewish	1911	----	Cmdr	Ukrain	1927-1930	1930-1957
MIKOYAN, Ansastas Ivonovich, 1895-1978							
Peas	Arm	1915	Theo	----	Krai	1926-1935	1935-1966
KHRUSHCHEV, Nitkita Sergeevich, 1894-1971							
Peas	Russ	1918	Poly	LtG	Oblast	1935-1939	1939-1964
MALENKOV, Georgii Maksimilianovich, 1902-							
Wkr?	Russ	1920	----	Cmdr	----	1941-1946	1946-1957
BULGANIN, Nikolai Aleksandrovich, 1895-1975							
Wkr?	Russ	1917	----	Mshl	----	1946-1948	1948-1958
PERVUKHIN, Mikhail Georgievich, 1904-1978							
Wkr?	Russ	1919	Eng	LtG	----	1957-1961	1952-1957
SABUROV, Maksim Zakharovich, 1900-							
Wkr?	Russ	1920	Inst	Cmdr	----	----	1952-1957
KIRICHENKO, Aleksey Illarionovich, 1908-1975							
Peas	Ukrain	1930	Eng	----	Ukrain	1953-1955	1955-1960
SUSLOV, Mikhail Andreevich (Reentry), 1902-1982							
Peas	Russ	1921	Ecn	Cmdr	Oblast	----	1952-1953 1955-1982
CANDIDATE MEMBERS ONLY DURING THE PERIOD							
BAGIROV, Mir Dzhafar Abbasovich, 1896-1956							
Wkr?	Azeri	1917	Univ	Cmdr Gen	----	1953-1953	----

* The key to the profile categories, including an explanation of the abbreviations used, can be found on pages 9-12.

Sect. or Org.[g]	Presidium Sup. Sov.[g]	Council of Ministers[g]	Other Important Experience	Travel Outside Bloc	Why Off Politb.	Cause of Death[h]
Yes	Yes	Pm	ForMin	Much	Expl	----
Yes	Prs	Yes	----	Some	Hlth	Ntrl
Yes	----	Yes	APG	----	Expl	----
----	Prs	Yes	----	Much	Hlth	Ntrl
Fst	----	Pm	----	Much	Hlth	Ntrl
IstSec	----	Pm	APG	Some	Expl	----
----	----	Pm	APG	Much	Expl	Ntrl
----	----	Yes	Amb Koms	Some	Rem	Ntrl
----	----	Yes	Gos Koms	Much	Rem	----
Yes	----	----	----	----	Rem	Ntrl
Yes	Yes	----	AgP	----	Rem	
Yes				Much	Died	Ntrl
----	Yes	----	MVD	----	Expl	Exec

Profile 7
THE KHRUSHCHEV POLITBURO, 1953-1956 (Continued)

a Family Back.	b Nation- ality	Year into Party	c Higher Ed.	d Military Exp.	e Repub. or Region 1st Sec	f Years Cand. Politburo or Presidium	f Years Full Politburo or Presidium
KABANOV, Ivan Grigor'evich, 1898-1972							
Wkr?	Russ?	Nd	Nd	Nd	Nd	1953-1958	----
MEL'NIKOV, Leonid Georgievich, 1906-1981							
Wkr?	Russ	1928	Poly	----	Ukrain	1953-1956	1952-1953
PEGOV, Nikolay Mikhaylovich, 1905-							
Wkr	Russ	1930	Acad	----	Krai	1953-1956	----
PONOMARENKO, Panteleimon Kondrat'evich, 1902-							
Wkr?	Russ	1925	Eng	Cmdr	Kazak	1953-1956	1952-1953
SHVERNIK, Nikolai Mikhailovich, 1888-1970							
Wkr?	Russ	1905	----	Cmdr	Oblast	1939-1952 1953-1957	1952-1953 1957-1964
YUDIN, Pavel Fedorovich, 1899-1968							
Peas	Russ	1918	Inst	Cmdr	----	1953-1959	----
BREZHNEV, Leonid Il'ich, 1906-1982							
Wkr?	Russ	1931	Eng	LtG	Kazak	1952-1953 1956-1957	1957-1982
FURTSEVA, Ekaterina Alekseevna, 1910-1974							
Wkr	Russ	1930	Poly	----	Gorod	1956-1957	1957-1961
MUKHITDINOV, Nuritdin Akramovich, 1917-							
Wkr	Uzb?	1942	Some	Cmdr	Uzb	1956-1957	1957-1961
SHEPILOV, Dmitrii Trofimovich, 1905-							
Wkr?	Russ?	1926	Ag Lw	MjG	----	1956-1957	----
ZHUKOV, Georgii Konstantinovich, 1896-1974							
Peas	Russ	1919	MilA	Mshl	----	1956-1957	1957-1957

Sect. or Org. [g]	Presidium Sup. Sov. [g]	Council of Ministers [g]	Other Important Experience	Travel Outside Bloc	Why Off Politb.	Cause of Death [h]
----	----	Yes	Nd	Nd	Rem	Ntrl
----	----	Yes	----	----	Rem	Ntrl
Yes	Yes	Yes	Amb Dip	Much	Rem	----
Yes	----	Yes	Amb Dip	MMuch	Rem	----
----	Prs	----	TU	Some	Rem	----
			TU	Some	Rem	Ntrl
----	----	----	Amb Hist Prof	----	Rem	Ntrl
Fst	Prs	Yes	----	Much	Ntrl	
Yes	----	Yes	CltMin	Much	Rem	Ntrl
Yes	----	----	Dip	Some	Rem	----
Yes	----	Yes	Ag APG APG	Much	Expl	----
----	----	Yes	DfMin	Much	Ntrl	

I conclude that a likely scenario is that since both Mikoyan and Voroshilov survived the 1957-58 purge of the "anti-party group" along with the two 1955 Khrushchev appointees, (5) Kirichenko (1955-60) and Suslov (1955-82, a returnee from the class of 1952), the four survivors must have persuaded Khrushchev that they had not supported the attempt to oust him. Perhaps, earlier in June, Voroshilov had been in sympathy with the ouster, but later backed off from such a position.

In light of the above, the numbers and names associated with the waltz macabre of 1957 unmask the probability that in one of the most extraordinary "votes" ever taken by the Politburo, Kaganovich (1930-57), Malenkov (1946-57), Molotov (1926-57), Pervukhin (1952-57) and Saburov (1952-57) voted for the ouster while Khrushchev's continued tenure was supported by the faithful four, with Khrushchev's vote a slim majority of 5 to 4, if Bulganin was absent. As noted above, the early June decision must have been taken while Bulganin (then Chairman of the Council of Ministers) and Khrushchev were on a state visit to Finland.

That among the offending five, Kaganovich, Malenkov and Molotov had been stalwart sycophants of Stalin's hardly seems accidental. I surmise from the demography of the 1957-58 ousters that the three were greatly offended by Khrushchev's "secret speech" of 1956. Quite possibly that event was what had triggered them to move as soon as they felt the time was ripe.

Where did Bulganin stand? He, of course, had been out of the country with Khrushchev when the original "anti-Party group" made their initial decision. However, the fact that he was ousted in 1958, one year after the rest of the "anti-Party group," underscores his later confession that indeed he had become a secret member of the opposition.

Perhaps the narrow margin of the "vote," vacillation among the opposition (especially by Bulganin and Voroshilov), plus the lack of any rules for leadership transition, was what allowed Khrushchev to play an unprecedented trump card. Through the timely aid of Zhukov (1957-57), who was rewarded by a short several months' tenure on the Politburo, military planes were used to bring the members of the Central Committee to Moscow from the far reaches of the empire for an extraordinary June plenary session of the Central Committee, at which Khrushchev received a vote of confidence. Then he moved to change the makeup of the Politburo.

Whatever the true course of events in 1957, the members of the 14-person body that existed during the whole of 1958 included Furtseva (1957-61), the first and only woman ever to be a member of the otherwise exclusive all-male Soviet college of cardinals. Among the rest were the faithful four Khrushchev incumbents, plus the eight new members of the quite unusual class of 1957. The only difference between the 1957 and 1958 Politburo was that Bulganin was removed in 1958.

Khrushchev's chess game repeats the basic Stalin pattern, but in addition to obtaining his unprecedented vote of confidence from the Central Committee, he employed still another new twist of his own. The nine 1957 inductees were actually older than the incumbents (58 vs. 54 years of age). What particularly marked them was the fact that the four oldest of the newcomers were retreads from the class of 1952. Apparently, during their brief earlier tenure they had impressed Khrushchev as patrons who would serve as his faithful allies. Khrushchev did not stop with his addition of full voting members. As seen in Profile 8, "The Khrushchev Politburo: 1957-63," in 1957 alone he added seven candidate members to the Politburo.

By 1958, having successfully employed the unwritten rules of elections Soviet style, Khrushchev had reached the zenith of his power. Sputnik's globe-circling beep the year before had sent a message to the world that indeed the USSR was a superpower in a position seriously to rival the United States colossus. Almost everything seemed to be going Khrushchev's way.

Turning to the composite measures of the 1953-56 Politburo recorded above, perhaps the most important difference between the 1957-63 period and the previous period is that Khrushchev was now an old man.

In 1957 Khrushchev turned 63, by 1963 he was 69. The average age of the Politburo in 1963 was 57.

During the period 1957-63, 20 incumbents served under Khrushchev. Their family origins were 55% peasant and 45% worker. The nationality composition was 70% Russian, 15% Ukrainian and other 15%. In terms of education 40% had had at least some higher education and another 40% had had polytechnical training.

Where previous experience is concerned, 80% had served, or were serving, as regional or republic Party first secretaries. When service as a candidate member of the Politburo is combined with that of having been on the 1952-53 Politburo, 90% had had such a Kremlin apprenticeship. Prior to, or during their time in office, 80% traveled outside of the Bloc.

Profile 8
THE KHRUSHCHEV POLITBURO, 1957-1963*

a Family Back.	b Nation-ality	Year into Party	c Higher Ed.	d Military Exp.	e Repub. or Region 1st Sec.	f Years Cand. Politburo or Presidium	f Years Full Politburo or Presidium
FULL VOTING MEMBERS							
MIKOYAN, Ansastas Ivonovich, 1895-1978							
Peas	Arm	1915	Theo	----	Krai	1926-1935	1935-1966
KHRUSHCHEV, Nikita Sergeevich, 1894-1971							
Peas	Russ	1918	Poly	LtG	Oblast	1935-1939	1939-1964
KIRICHENKO, Aleksey Illarionovich, 1908-1975							
Peas	Ukrain	1930	Eng	----	Ukrain	1953-1955	1955-1960
SUSLOV, Mikhail Andreevich (Reentry), 1902-1982							
Peas	Russ	1921	Ecn	Cmdr	Oblast	----	1952-1953 1955-1982
ARISTOV, Averkii Borisovich (Reentry), 1903-1973							
Wkr?	Russ	1921	Poly	----	Oblast	----	1952-1953 1957-1961
BELYAEV, Nikolai Il'ich, 1903-1966							
Peas	Russ?	1921	Ecn	----	Krai	----	1957-1960
BREZHNEV, Leonid Il'ich, 1906-1982							
Wkr?	Russ	1931	Eng	LtG	Kazak	1952-1953	1957-1982
FURTSEVA, Ekaterina Alekseevna, 1910-1974							
Wkr	Russ	1930	Poly	----	Gorod	1956-1957	1957-1961
IGNATOV, Nikolai Grigor'evich, 1901-1966							
Peas	Russ	1924	PolA	----	Oblast	1952-1953	1957-1961
KOZLOV, Frol Romanovich, 1908-1965							
Peas	Russ	1926	Poly	----	Oblast	1957-1957	1957-1964
KUUSINEN, Otto Vil'gel'movich, 1881-1964							
Wkr?	Fin	1904	Univ	cmdr	----	----	1952-1953 1957-1964
MUKHITDINOV, Nuritdin Akramovich, 1917-							
Wkr	Uzb?	1942	Some	Cmdr	Uzb	1956-1957	1957-1961
SHVERNIK, Nikolai Mikhailovich, 1888-1970							
Wkr?	Russ	1905	----	Cmdr	Oblast	1939-1952 1953-1957	1952-1953 1957-1964

* The key to the profile categories, including an explanation of the abbreviations used, can be found on pages 9-12.

Sect. or Org. [g]	Presidium Sup. Sov. [g]	Council of Ministers [g]	Other Important Experience	Travel Outside Bloc	Why Off Politb.	Cause of Death [h]
----	Prs	Yes	----	Much	Hlth	Ntrl
Fst	----	Pm	----	Much	Hlth	Ntrl
Yes	----	----	----	----	Rem	Ntrl
Yes	Yes	----	AgP	----	Rem	----
Yes				Much	Died	Ntrl
----	----	----	Koms TU	----	Rem	----
Yes			Amb	Some	Rem	Ntrl
Yes	Yes	----	----	----	Rem	Ntrl
Fst	Prs	Yes	----	Much	Died	Ntrl
Yes	----	Yes	CltMin	Much	Rem	Ntrl
Yes	----	Yes	----	----	Rem	Ntrl
Yes	Yes	Yes	----	----	Hlth	Ntrl
----	Yes	----	Prs KarFin	Some	Rem	----
Yes				Some	Died	Ntrl
Yes	----	----	Dip	Some	Rem	----
----	Prs	----	TU	Some	Rem	----
			TU	Some	Rem	Ntrl

Profile 8
THE KHRUSHCHEV POLITBURO, 1957-1963 (Continued)

a Family Back.	b Nation-ality	Year into Party	c Higher Ed.	d Military Exp.	e Repub. or Region 1st Sec	f Years Cand. Politburo or Presidium	f Years Full Politburo or Presidium
ZHUKOV, Georgii Konstantinovich, 1896-1974							
Peas	Russ	1919	MilA	Mshl	----	1956-1957	1957-1957
KOSYGIN, Aleksey Nikolaevich, 1904-1980							
Wkr?	Russ	1927	Poly	----	----	1946-1948	1948-1952
PODGORNY, Nikolai Viktorovich, 1903-							
Wkr?	Ukrain	1930	Poly	----	Ukrain	1958-1960	1960-1977
POLYANSKY, Dmitrii Steepanivich, 1917-							
Peas	Ukrain	1939	Poly	----	Oblast	1958-1960	1960-1976
VORONOV, Gennadii Ivanovich, 1910-							
Peas	Russ	1931	PolA	----	Oblast	1961-1961	1961-1973
KIRILENKO, Andrei Pavlovich, 1906-							
Peas	Russ	1931	Poly	Cmdr	Oblast	1957-1961	1962-1982
CANDIDATE MEMBERS ONLY DURING THE PERIOD							
KALNBERZIN, Yan Eduardovich, 1893-							
Wkr?	Lat	1917	Univ	Cmdr	Lat	1957-1961	----
MAZUROV, Kirill Trofimovich, 1914-							
Peas	Bel	1940	Poly	Cmdr	Bel	1957-1965	1965-1978
MZHAVANDADZE, Vasilii Pavlovich, 1902-							
Wkr?	Georg	1927	MilA	LtG	Georg	1957-1972	----
PERVUKHIN, Mikhail Georgievich, 1904-1978							
Wkr?	Russ	1919	Eng	LtG	----	1957-1961	1952-1957
POSPELOV, Petr Nikolaevich, 1898-1979							
Wkr?	Russ	1916	PolA	----	----	1957-1961	----
PUZANOV, Aleksandr Mikhailovich, 1906-							
Peas	Russ	1925	Poly	----	Oblast	1957-1962	----
GRISHIN, Viktor Vasil'evich, 1914-							
Wkr	Russ	1939	Poly	----	Gorod	1961-1971	1971-

g Sect. or Org.	g Pre- sidium Sup. Sov.	g Council of Ministers	Other Important Experience	Travel Outside Bloc	Why Off Politb.	h Cause of Death
----	----	Yes	DfMin	Much	Expl	Ntrl
----	----	Yes Pm	Gos	Much Much	Rem Hlth	---- Ntrl
Yes	Prs	----	----	Some	Rem	----
----	----	Yes	Ag Amb	Some	Rem	----
Yes	----	Yes	Ag	Some	Rem	----
Yes	----	----	----	Little	Rem?	----
----	----	----	----	----	Rem	----
----	----	----	----	Some	Hlth	----
----	----	----	Dip	Some	Hlth	----
----	----	Yes	Amb Koms	Some	Rem	Ntrl
Yes	----	----	Ag Hist Prof DrMLI EdPrv	----	Rem	Ntrl
Yes	----	----	Ag Amb Dip	Much	Rem	----
----	Yes	----	----	Much	----	----

Profile 8
THE KHRUSHCHEV POLITBURO, 1957-1963 (Continued)

a Family Back.	b Nation-ality	Year into Party	c Higher Ed.	d Military Exp.	e Repub. or Region 1st Sec	f Years Cand. Politburo or Presidium	f Years Full Politburo or Presidium
RASHIDOV, Sharaf Rashidovich, 1917-							
Wkr?	Uzb	1939	Ped	Cmdr	Uzb	1961-1984	----
SHCHERBITSKY, Vladimir Vasil'evich, 1918-							
Wkr	Ukrain	1941	Poly	Cmdr	Ukrain	1961-1963	1971-
EFREMOV, Leonid Nikolaevich (sometimes spelled Yefremov), 1912-							
Wkr?	Russ	?Nd	Nd	Nd	Oblast	1962-1966	----
SHELEST, Petr Efimovich, 1908-							
Wkr?	Ukrain	1928	Poly	----	Oblast	1963-1964 1965-1971	1964-1973

g Sect. or Org.	g Pre- sidium Sup. Sov.	g Council of Ministers	Other Important Experience	Travel Outside Bloc	Why Off Politb.	h Cause of Death
----	----	----	Dip Teach	Much	Rem	----
----	----	Yes	----	Little	----	----
----	----	----	----	----	Rem	----
----	----	----	Dip	Some	Rem	----

Among those who are known to have died since, the average lifespan was 72 years. The average time the incumbents served on the Politburo was 14 years. Expulsion and/or removal from the Politburo accounts for 60% of the exits from the Politburo, while the rest either died in office or retired for health reasons.

Table 9 compares composite demographic measures of the Khrushchev 1957-63 Politburo with those for his 1953-56 Poliburo and with the Stalin 1946-51 Politburo.

As the change-index reveals, largely reflecting the 1957 shakeup, 1957-63 was the most unstable of all of the Politburo periods.

Moreover, the personnel changes engineered by Khrushchev involved one of the most momentous changes that have occurred in the evolution of that body.

If the sub-periods identified in this study had been determined solely by the numbers generated in the change-index 1960 (index = +27) and/or 1961 (index = + 22) would have been identified as the start of another sub-period within the Khrushchev era. In fact, we may be wrong and future research and analysis will identify those years as an important time of change in the post-Stalin years. However, as I have tried to stress, although I believe that the numbers generated by the change-index are an important guide to Politburo affairs, they have not been the only factors contributing to the judgements made here.

As documented in Profile 8, "The Khrushchev Politburo: 1957-63," in 1960 three new full members were added. They were: Kosygin (for a second term, 1948-52 and 1960-80), Podgorny (1960-77), and Polyansky (1960-76), while Kirichenko (1955-60) and Belyaev (1957-60) were removed. Voronov (1961-73) was the only full voting member added in 1961, a year when Aristov (1952-53 and again 1957-61), Furtseva (1957-61), Ignatov (1957-61) and Mukhitdinov (1957-61) were removed. Perhaps I am wrong, but the fact that five of the six members removed in 1960 and 1961 had entered in 1957 suggests the possibility that the high rate of change at that time was a hangover from the events of 1957, at a time (1960 and 1961) when Khrushchev was still in full command of the Politburo. Of course, there is another possible scenario. Perhaps Khrushchev already had sensed serious opposition among his colleagues and the bloodless purge of the Politburo in 1960-61 was an early attempt on his part to abort his dismissal, which was to come in 1964. While the second possible explanation is not necessarily incompatible with the first (i.e., there may be merit in both), the second scenario more closely fits with Alexander Yanov's very persuasive analysis of the events of the early 1960s.

Table 9

COMPOSITE MEASURES OF MEANS OF POLITBURO PERIODS: 1946-63*

	1946-51	1953-56	1957-63
Number on Politburo	11	10	13
The change-index	-8	+2	+16
% off from previous year (a)	3	16	17
% off health reasons (b)	3	2	0
% new (c)	8	5	14
Age Frst. Sec. first year	67	59	63
Politburo means			
Age	55	59	59
Total years served (d)	13	14	7
Origins in %			
Peasant	64	60	55
Worker	30	40	45
Intellectual	6	0	0
Russian	64	75	68
Ukrainian	0	5	12
Other Nationality	36	20	20
Education in %			
Some higher	3	29	41
Polytechnical	33	16	39
Experience in %			
Regional Frst. Sec.	23	25	64
Republic Frst. Sec	17	15	19
Apprenticeship (e)	82	80	94
Secretariat	67	60	74
Presidium Sup. Sov.	46	30	33
Council of Ministers	100	91	56
Travel outside Bloc (f)	57	85	83

*Means for all of the years within each of the periods.

a-The percentage of the previous year's Politburo that is not returned, b-the percentage of the previous year's Politburo not returned for health reasons, c-the percentage of that year's Politburo that is new, d-years served at that point in time, e-previous service either as a candidate or full Politburo member, f-excluding travel prior to 1917.

As I will elaborate on more fully later (with Yanov's analysis as partial documentation) 1960 and 1961 were precisely the years that Khrushchev moved massively against the first secretaries at the provincial level. The power base for most of the Kremlin leaders rests upon their provincial clients. All of the Politburo members removed in 1960 and 1961 had come from successful tours as oblast, krai, gorod or republic first secretaries. Perhaps, their major sin was to oppose the major shakeup that Khrushchev was making in his "failed reform" of the Party in the early 1960s. (6)

The Soviet Union is a major industrial power. More than anything else, modern industrial powers are dependent upon knowledge and information. However street-wise political leaders may be, much of their success is determined by their ability to exploit the human knowledge reservoir present in their society. Moreover, uneducated leaders are not normally equipped to judge who among the experts and specialists are the most knowledgeable and wise, to be kept on tap to advise the leaders in their decision making. Surely, then, it was inevitable that the educational level of the members of the Politburo was destined to increase dramatically over that which prevailed under Stalin's leadership. Nevertheless, I submit that what was preordained does not wholly explain the fact that by far the greatest increase in the history of the Politburo in the level of education of its members occurred under Khrushchev.

In the 1946-52 period only 3% of the Stalin Politburo had been exposed to some form of advanced training. In contrast during the final period of Khrushchev's rule 41% had had such training. Moreover, among the 17 individuals inducted into the Politburo under Khrushchev, 16 had had either higher or polytechnical training --53% higher and 41% polytechnical. (7) Shvernik (1957-64), a retread from the class of 1952, was the only exception. His major expertise lay in his long service as the Soviet trade union chief.

Khrushchev himself was largely self-educated. However, quite unlike Stalin and perhaps more than any of his successors, one of Khrushchev's major attributes was intellectual curiosity. Unfortunately, his knowledge gaps often gave him trouble --e.g., during much of his rule he supported the charlatan biologist Lysenko. Nevertheless, he did go to great effort to obtain expert advice as exemplified by his turning to the American seed corn pioneer Roswell Garst.

Khrushchev's quest for knowledge that would help advance Soviet life must also be a major explanation for the significant expansion of travel by both Soviet specialists and fellow Politburo members during his time in office.

As noted earlier, the all-time record harvest of 1958 led Khrushchev to proclaim that henceforth grain would be plentiful. Earlier that year, probably little related to the prospects of the harvest, Khrushchev decreed the abolishment of the MTS. Not only were the stations no longer needed to control the farms, but by mandatory sales of the state-owned machinery to the collectives, Moscow could recoup much of what Khrushchev obviously believed was an over investment in farming. The rubles saved could be used for industrial and military expansion.

What Khrushchev failed to see was that the new lands fields could not produce enough additional grain, particularly feed grains, to meet the citizens' increasing dietary demand, especially for more meat on the table. However, responding to that demand, he also put out a call to grow corn, almost everywhere. Unfortunately, very little Soviet land has the combination of warmth and moisture necessary to cultivate the "queen of the fields" satisfactorily. That scheme too was a failure and sometimes in private, Khrushchev was derisively referred to as "kukuruznik," the "corn chap." (8)

Certainly, Khrushchev's personality faults embarrassed many Soviet officials. His shakeup of the ministries, attempt to reorganize regional administration along the lines of territorial-production administrations (the sovnarkhozy), and his educational reforms were rather hairbrained and futile. Moreover his schemes threatened a major segment of the bureaucratic hierarchy.

Khrushchev's campaign in the countryside in the early 1960s solidified the prefects against him. According to Yanov that fact was to be a major factor in Khrushchev's downfall. Thus, in 1960-61 alone he presided over the dismissal of "more than half" of the district first secretaries in the Russian and Ukrainian republics. Yanov records the response of a Dagestan rayon first secretary as follows: "'No Tsar ever gave up his power voluntarily, and I don't intend to give mine up without a fight.'"(9)

All of the above, plus more and, especially, three major events that occurred early in the 1960s undermined the confidence in Khrushchev's rule.

The open rupture with China was a major blow to Soviet egos and the hope that Moscow was the model for the future world. In 1962 President Kennedy proved that Khrushchev and company had recklessly attempted to overextend Soviet power. Most of all, however, just as weather has been such a crucial factor in shaping Russian and Soviet military history, I believe that the unfavorable weather of 1963 sealed Khrushchev's fate.

The 1963 crop failure necessitated the slaughter of a third of the nation's hogs. Moreover, for the first time in all of the history of Russia and the Soviet Union, the nation became a major commercial importer of grain. Khrushchev's principal claim to domestic success rested on his agricultural policies, and the weather proved that they were a miserable failure.

The Khrushchev Legacy

Although some of the reforms Khrushchev attempted to make were destined to fail (e.g., in education and some of his agricultural schemes), no period in Soviet history between the mid-1930s and 1985 witnessed more change than that which occurred during his eleven years at the helm. Therefore, prior to examining the post-Khrushchev period, an insight into what was to come can be gained by looking at some of the more important post-1953 trends in Soviet political and economic affairs, changes that largely are a legacy of the Khrushchev era.

The differences between the Stalin and post-Stalin Politburos are illuminated in Table 10 which compares composite measures of the 1917-52 Politburos with the measures of the 1953-85 Politburos.

Most of the numbers generated in our comparisons of the two major periods in Soviet Politburo history will not surprise close students of Soviet politics. However, some of the comparisons are revealing.

The most surprising finding to this writer is the relative scores on the change-index. Prior to doing the study, very cognizant of the upheavals on the Politburo in the early years (especially during the Stalin purges), I would have asserted confidently that the pre-1953 Politburos were less stable than those that have existed since 1952. However, our change-index reveals just the opposite. The score for the 36-year period 1917-52, even including the major shakeup in 1952, is a -2, while the score, for the 33 post-1952 years is a +2. Let me remind the reader again that the higher the index score the greater the turnover for other than health reasons.

Table 10

COMPOSITE MEASURES OF MEANS OF POLITBURO PERIODS: 1917-52 vs. 1953-85

	1917-52	1953-85
Number on Politburo	9	13
The change-index	-2	+2
% off from previous year (a)	8	11
% off health reasons (b)	2	3
% new (c)	10	9
Age Frst. Sec. first year	47	59
Politburo means		
Age	48	62
Total years served (d)	7	8
Origins in %		
Peasant	50	46
Worker	30	49
Intellectual	20	5
Russian	59	64
Ukrainian	1	17
Other Nationality	40	19
Education in %		
Some higher	26	45
Polytechnical	13	43
Experience in %		
Regional Frst. Sec.	17	46
Republic Frst. Sec.	11	27
Apprenticeship (e)	55	85
Secretariat	68	56
Presidium Sup. Sov.	56	34
Council of Ministers	77	54
Travel outside Bloc (f)	44	90

*Means for all of the years within each of the periods.

a-The percentage of the previous year's Politburo that is not returned, b-the percentage of the previous year's Politburo not returned for health reasons, c-the percentage of that year's Politburo that is new, d-years served at that point in time, e-previous service either as a candidate or full Politburo member, f-excluding travel prior to 1917.

Clearly, if one were to devise an index of rough treatment after removal, the scores would be the other way around. Many of the Politburo members in the earlier period wound up being imprisoned and/or executed, while Beriya is the only Politburo member since 1952 to suffer such a fate. Nevertheless, Politburo politics is a serious game and, as indicated, if anything, removal from that body against the member's will has slightly accelerated, certainly it has not decreased. As indicated previously, the mean age of the members has increased significantly.

There have been important shifts in the ethnic makeup of the body, but not at the expense of the Russians, whose representation has actually increased. Finally, the Ukrainians, who are the second largest nationality in the USSR, are now represented. (10)

Higher education has become important and, as the reader will see, the trend is for it to become even more important in the future.

Experience as either a regional or a republic first secretary is more important than prior to 1953 and, especially, service as an apprentice candidate member has become most important for elevation to full Politburo membership.

Finally, no longer is it true that a majority of the Politburo members have not journeyed outside of the Soviet bloc. Now, travel abroad is part of the package of Soviet leadership experience.

The measures offered in Table 8 (above) for the years identified as the beginning of the sub-periods suggest the existence of several trends that deserve further exploration when the composite numbers for the various post-1952 periods that have been identified are examined. (See Table 15 below) The trends are:

1. As measured by the change index, Politburo membership has become more stable since the major upheaval in 1957. However, since the degree of turnover can be associated with policy changes, the relatively high index score for 1985 suggests that Gorbachev has been lining up the votes for important policy changes in the near future.

2. Although the mean age of the Politburo may dip slightly in the early years of Gorbachev's leadership, it seems destined to remain near or above 66.

3. Perhaps, largely reflecting changes in Soviet demographics as a whole, there is a trend for peasant origin to become less important, while

worker origin is more important, for becoming a Politburo member. Similarly, reflecting the increased level of education of the population as a whole and the huge size of the post-war bureaucracy, one can project that more and more members of the Politburo in the future will be drawn from those whose parents can be classified as intellectuals, hardly as ordinary peasants or workers.

4. Although the Russians remain overrepresented on the Politburo, they no longer dominate that body to the degree they once did.

5. The time when the Politburo was dominated by those without at least some advanced educational training is gone. Therefore, in future years higher education will be an increasingly important prerequisite for Politburo membership.

6. Having successfully served as either a regional or a republic first secretary (often those who have done the latter have done both) remains an important requirement for advancement to the top rung of Soviet political power.

7. Apprenticeship as a candidate Politburo member increasingly is a requirement for full membership.

8. Simultaneous or previous service on the Council of Ministers or on the Presidium of the Supreme Soviet remains important for Politburo members, although service on the Council of Ministers may be less important than it was earlier.

9. Travel outside of the bloc has become an essential activity for the top leaders of the Soviet superpower. Indeed, the only member of the Gorbachev Politburo who as yet has not had such experience is Cherbrikov who, of course, is the head of the KGB.

Finally, in our examination of the Khrushchev legacy there is one other source of demographic comparisons between the pre- and post-1952 periods that deserves examination. What distinguishes the 30 individuals who have served as candidate Politburo members only from those who have achieved full voting status? (See Table 11.)

Table 11

FULL VS. CANDIDATE ONLY DEMOGRAPHICS: 1917-52 VS. 1953-85*

	1917-52		1953-85	
	Full	Cand-idate only	Full	Cand-idate only
Total during periods	49	12	40	18
Origins in %				
Peasant	50	33	46	16
Worker	30	67	49	67
Intellectual	20	6	5	16
Russian	59	50	64	67
Ukrainian	1	25	17	0
Other nationality	40	25	19	33
Education in %				
Some higher	26	25	45	83
Polytechnical	13	25	43	17
Experience in %				
Regional Frst. Sec.	17	33	46	27
Republic Frst. Sec.	11	17	27	27
Secretariat	68	25	56	39
Presidium Sup. Sov.	56	25	34	22
Council of Ministers	77	58	54	27
Travel outside Bloc **	44	25	90	50

*Means for all of the years within each of the periods.

**Excluding travel prior to 1917.

Perhaps Sokolov, who was elevated to a candidate position only in 1985, will be awarded full membership later, but given his age in 1985 (74) this seems unlikely. On the other hand Talyzin, who also was raised to candidate membership in 1985, probably will receive full status later, since he was only 56 that year. Table 11 reveals some important demographic differences between the 89 incumbents who achieved full membership and the 30 who have fallen into the also-ran category.

As shown in Table 11, both before and after 1952, when compared with the full voting members, a much greater percentage of the candidate members came from worker rather than peasant origins. Since, but not prior to 1952, more of the candidates have come from intellectual homes, and their level of higher educational exposure has been much higher. This, of course, supports the identification of a trend among the full members, for that body to be made up increasingly of individuals with intellectual origins who have had higher education.

Not surprisingly, significantly fewer of the candidate-only members have simultaneously held other high state positions.

Perhaps the most interesting revelation found in the comparison of the candidate only members with the full members is that, since 1952, whereas the Ukrainian nationality has been well represented on the full-voting Politburo (17%), the other minority nationalities find their place as candidate members, 33% of that group. In sum, while not ignored, excluding the Ukrainians who now are generously represented on the full voting Politburo, the other minority nationalities are present among the central leaders, but largely at the non-voting level.

NOTES

1. PRAVDA, December 25, 1961, pp. 1-4.

2. Michael Kort, THE SOVIET COLOSSUS: A HISTORY OF THE USSR, New York: Charles Scribner's Sons, 1985, p. 246.

3. Alec Nove, STALINISM AND AFTER, London: George Allen & Unwin Ltd., 1975, p. 139.

4. Roy A. Medvedev and Zhores A. Medvedev, KHRUSHCHEV THE YEARS IN POWER, (Trans. by Andrew R. Durkin), New York: W. W. Norton & Company, 1978, p. 76.

5. True, Voroshilov was retired for "health" reasons in 1960, when he was 79. Mikoyan, however, outlasted Khrushchev and did not leave the Politburo until 1966.

6. Alexander Yanov, THE DRAMA OF THE SOVIET 1960S: A LOST REFORM, Berkeley: University of California Institute of International Studies, 1984, pp. 38-47.

7. As discussed earlier, some might quarrel with the definitions employed here in determining who fell into which of the two education categories. Therefore, the judgements used need further explanation. As far as polytechnical training was concerned, that choice was relatively easy --e.g., the individual learned to be a machinist in a polytechnical school. Those classified as having at least some higher education include individuals who attended a college, university, institute, a military academy or one of the Party's political academies, where I presume the training was not solely confined to studying Marxism-Leninism.

8. In 1960, just prior to my first visit to the rural USSR, I spent a weekend in Coon Rapids, Iowa talking to Roswell Garst about corn and Khrushchev. Two strong impressions that I gained from the visit with Garst were: Garst was a superb salesman who could have convinced an eskimo to grow corn in the Arctic. Garst did not appreciate the enormous power and authority held by Khrushchev and the fact that, unlike his American customers, Soviet farmers plant what when and how largely in response to Moscow's dictates. In sum, Khrushchev became Garst and Thomas Company's Soviet super salesman who cajoled, indeed virtually commanded, Soviet farmers to plant corn almost up to the edge of the Arctic circle. The results were nearly disastrous.

9. Yanov, Op. Cit., p. 73.

10. Not only do the Ukrainians comprise the second largest nationality group, but prior to the opening of the new lands in the 1950s, the Ukraine was "the breadbasket of Russia." The Ukraine was far from ignored in terms of Politburo membership prior to 1953, but the representatives were not Ukrainian nationals, they were Russians and others who had served as key administrators in the republic which had tried to break away and become independent after 1917. For example, although Kaganovich was born in the Ukraine and spoke the language, he came from a Jewish family. He served as first secretary of the Ukraine from 1928 to 1939.

6

The Brezhnev Era (1964–81)

The setting for Brezhnev's entry onto the scene needs to be put in the perspective of the Khrushchev exit. Did Khrushchev go out fighting in 1964, or did his colleagues convince him that this time around he really did not have the votes and ought to retire for reasons of "health"?

Prior to this analysis of the evolving demographics of the Politburo I was persuaded that, while not bloody, Khrushchev's ouster must have been very traumatic. Surely, it was a serious blow to Khrushchev himself. However, among the twelve 1963 incumbents, only Khrushchev, Kozlov (1957-64) and Kuusinen (1957-64) exited in 1964. True, the two Khrushchev colleagues had been star members of the class of 1957, but, more importantly, I submit, Kuusinen died in 1964 and, surely in bad health, Kozlov died the next year. Further, although Shelepin (1964-75) and Shelest (1964-73) were added in 1964, their additions only maintained the Politburo at a count of 11, one less than it had been in 1963.

When the 1964 changes are compared to the earlier, surely more extensive, shakeups in the Politburo at times of a challenge to the leadership, or leadership transition (i.e., 1926, 1952-53, and 1957), in light of the 1964 demographic changes, one may hypothesize that this time around Khrushchev was faced with overwhelming opposition, which, wisely, he chose not to fight. Again, in addition to his personality shortcomings, especially his repetition of the Stalin fault of encouraging a "personality cult," the Sino-Soviet split, the Cuban retreat and the disastrous grain harvest of 1963 had made evident that both his major international and domestic policies were seriously flawed.

When contrasted to the earlier challenge and the earlier changes in leadership, the class of 1964 does not stand out. Moreover, Khrushchev was destined to live another seven years and, unprecedentedly, write his memoirs.

Not only did the memoirs survive, but they were "allowed" to leave the USSR. Why? Surely, had the Brezhnev Politburo so wished, Khrushchev's recollections never would have survived his pen. The memoirs, while anti-Stalin, are emphatically not anti-Soviet.

Could one motive for the unofficial release of the memoirs have been a message to the outside world that, along with other changes, Kremlin politics had evolved into a more civilized, less grim enterprise? In his introduction to the memoirs, Edward Crankshaw astutely points out that no one "active" in office while Khrushchev was writing was "attacked directly" in the book. More importantly, related to our hypothesis about a message to the West, Crankshaw speculates that their release may have been meant "to counter the current [late 1960s] attempts to rehabilitate Stalin." (1)

Act I: Damage Control and "Developed Socialism" (1964-72)

Internationally and domestically, Brezhnev instituted damage control to repair the faults of Khrushchev's rule.

In his speeches Brezhnev made clear that he believed the future belonged to the USSR, but not much reading between the lines was needed to learn that before the ultimate goal of world communism could be realized, significant internal Soviet advances needed to be achieved.

At the peak of his confidence that the future was at hand, Khrushchev had pronounced that the USSR had achieved the initial stage of communism. More modestly, Brezhnev scaled down that boast, stating that what had been achieved was "developed socialism." Moreover, he turned serious attention to improving living standards.

At no other period in Soviet history did the citizen's material welfare improve as much as it did during the last half of Khrushchev's rule and the first half of the Brezhnev era. However, a major price paid for that reform was a reduction in the rate of overall economic growth. Too late, at the end of his rule, Khrushchev had started to move in some of the directions that Brezhnev was to follow.

In the crucial realm of agriculture, Khrushchev had adopted policies that discouraged peasant private plot production. Brezhnev moved in the opposite direction. Most important of all, unprecedentedly in Soviet history, under Brezhnev massive new investments were poured into the countryside. Peasant incomes were advanced and more chemical aids and machinery were made available. By far the greatest increases in food availability occurred during the first half of Brezhnev's tenure in office.

As shown in Table 12, "Grain and Meat Production: 1960-85," up to that time, grain production had reached an all-time peak in 1964, a very good year when the Soviet fields produced some 671 kilograms of grain per capita. In 1970, also a good year, another new record of 773 kilograms of grain per capita was attained. Overall, Brezhnev had reason to believe that significant improvement was being made. However, he never made the mistake of proclaiming that the Soviet grain problem had been solved.

In the international realm, although marred by the Czech uprising in 1968 which precipitated the enunciation of the Brezhnev doctrine, the Brezhnev era was marked largely by the pursuit of peaceful coexistence, later elevated to the seemingly loftier idea of detente.

Although Soviet peace policies carried an element of expansionism, particularly in the third world (e.g., Africa and Southeast Asia), I submit that Brezhnev's foreign policy was formulated with the primary goal of improving the domestic situation, particularly in the economic realm.

One clear impression that surfaces from a review of Kremlin political demographics is that domestic concerns constitute the most important driving force. True, by far the most stable years for the Politburo were the World War II years, but even that period in Soviet history can be seen as largely domestically determined by a concentration of all effort, single-mindedly, on preserving the system, the empire and, most importantly, the lives and careers of its top leaders. Surely, had Hitler won the war, a German version of the Nürnberg trials would have cost the lives of Stalin and any other of his surviving Politburo colleagues.

Not only have domestic concerns dominated Politburo politics but, adhering to the political law that sensible foreign policies primarily are an extension of domestic needs and policies, shifts in Soviet foreign policy can be seen to be rooted primarily in domestic concerns. Therefore, the initiation of peaceful coexistence, and later detente, in the post-Stalin era can be seen largely as arising out of internal Soviet concerns. The turn away from Stalinist autarky witnessed an admission that the Soviet citizens' dietary demands necessitated the importation of massive amounts of grain. Similarly, acquiring Western scientific knowledge and technical equipment allowed the Soviet budget to avoid the enormous expense of reinventing the wheels of the modern high-technology age.

Table 12

GRAIN AND MEAT PRODUCTION: 1960-85

	Grain				Meat	
Year	(tons)*	Output per Capita (kgs.)	Import Export Balance (tons)*	Grain Imported	(tons)*	Output per Capita (kgs.)
1960	125.5	591	-6.56	-6.56	8.7	41
1961	130.8	605	-6.82	-6.82	8.7	40
1962	140.2	637	-7.75	-7.75	9.5	43
1963	107.5	481	-3.20	-3.20	10.2	46
1964	152.1	671	3.77	3.77	8.3	37
1965	121.1	527	2.04	2.04	10.0	44
1966	171.2	737	4.19	4.19	10.7	46
1967	147.9	630	-4.06	-4.06	11.5	49
1968	169.5	715	-3.80	-3.80	11.6	49
1969	162.4	678	-6.57	-6.55	11.6	48
1970	186.8	773	-3.54	-3.54	12.3	51
1971	181.2	743	-5.10	-5.10	13.2	54
1972	168.2	683	20.50	22.80	13.6	55
1973	222.5	895	5.20	11.30	13.5	54
1974	195.6	780	0.40	5.70	14.6	58
1975	140.1	553	25.40	26.10	15.0	59
1976	223.8	876	7.70	11.00	13.6	53
1977	195.7	759	16.60	18.90	14.7	57
1978	237.4	913	12.80	15.60	15.3	59
1979	179.2	683	30.00	31.00	15.5	59
1980	189.1	715	34.30	34.80	15.1	57
1981	160.0	600	45.60	46.00	15.2	57
1982	180.0	670	32.00	32.50	15.4	57
1983	190.0	701	32.40	32.70	16.4	60
1984	170.0	621	54.90	55.50	17.0	62
1985	190.0	688	38.90	35.00	--	--

Sources: NARODNOE KHOZYAISTVO SSSR, Moskva: Statistika, 1961 through 1983, SSSR V TSIFRAKH, Moskva: Statistika, 1984 and USSR GRAIN SITUATION AND OUTLOOK: FOREIGN AGRICULTURE CIRCULAR, Washington, D.C.: USDA FAS, since 1981.

*Million. Since 1981 official Soviet grain production data has not been published. Therefore, the grain data here for the years 1981-85 are based upon USDA estimates and projections.

Without external inputs, instead of just slowing, as it has, Soviet economic growth probably would have come to a halt and, especially, given quantities of feed grains imported, standards of living might well have declined.

Given the above as the basis for a hypothesis as to what forces govern Politburo politics, I submit that too often external viewers of Kremlin affairs have credited international factors with carrying more weight than they do. Thus, I posit that Politburo changes overwhelmingly are influenced by Soviet internal affairs. Not the least of such influences are who on the Politburo gets what, when and how. Public opinion is not ignored by members of the Politburo, but rarely does it influence directly promotion of their careers. Certainly, winning votes at the next election is not a concern of men who owe their high positions to patronage and cooptation into office.

Table 13 compares the demographic measures of the first Brezhnev Politburo with those of earlier Politburos.

The record as far as candidate members during the period will support what has been said above. During the whole period Brezhnev only added five candidate members, two of whom who were elevated to full membership in 1971, and the other three would attain full status at a later date, including Andropov (1973-84) who, of course, was destined to succeed Brezhnev as first secretary. See Profile 9 "The Brezhnev Politburo: 1964-72."

Not surprisingly the change-index for the 1964-72 period is negative. Moreover, according to the other measures I have used, this was one of the most stable of the Politburo periods. Little was changed from the previous Khrushchev period, other than that the bumptious Khrushchev was replaced by Brezhnev, the Soviet Union's number one bureaucrat.

Act II: Calm at the Helm (1973-81)

Dividing the history of a nation into periods always involves an element of artificiality, even though such an exercise can be of help in understanding changes that occurred. Dividing the Brezhnev era into the two parts that I have may result in more distortions than any of our previous divisions of leadership rule.

Profile 9
THE BREZHNEV POLITBURO, 1964-1972*

a Family Back.	b Nationality	Year into Party	c Higher Ed.	d Military Exp.	e Repub. or Region 1st Sec.	f Years Cand.	f Years Full
						Politburo or Presidium	
FULL VOTING MEMBERS							
MIKOYAN, Ansastas Ivonovich, 1895-1978							
Peas	Arm	1915	Theo	----	Krai	1926-1935	1935-1966
SUSLOV, Mikhail Andreevich (Reentry), 1902-1982							
Peas	Russ	1921	Ecn	Cmdr	Oblast	----	1952-1953 1955-1982
BREZHNEV, Leonid Il'ich, 1906-1982							
Wkr?	Russ	1931	Eng	LtG	Kazak	1952-1953 1956-1957	1957-1982
KOSYGIN, Aleksey Nikolaevich, 1904-1980							
Wkr?	Russ	1927	Poly	----	----	1946-1948 1957-1960	1948-1952 1960-1980
PODGORNY, Nikolai Viktorovich, 1903-							
Wkr?	Ukrain	1930	Poly	----	Ukrain	1958-1960	1960-1977
POLYANSKY, Dmitrii Stepanivich, 1917-							
Peas	Ukrain	1939	Poly	----	Oblast	1958-1960	1960-1976
VORONOV, Gennadii Ivanovich, 1910-							
Peas	Russ	1931	PolA	----	Oblast	1961-1961	1961-1973
KIRILENKO, Andrei Pavlovichk 1906-							
Peas	Russ	1931	Poly	Cmdr	Oblast	1957-1961	1962-1982
SHELEPIN, Aleksandr Nikolaevich, 1918-							
Wkr?	Russ	1940	Inst	Cmdr	----	----	1964-1975
SHELEST, Petr Efimovich, 1908-							
Wkr?	Ukrain	1928	Poly	----	Oblast	1963-1964	1964-1973
MAZUROV, Kirill Trofimovich, 1914-							
Peas	Bel	1940	Poly	Cmdr	Bel	1957-1965	1965-1978
PEL'SHE, Arvid Yanovich, 1899-1984							
Wkr?	Lat	1915	PolA	Cmdr	Lat	----	1966-1982
GRISHIN, Viktor Vasil'evich, 1914-							
Wkr	Russ	1939	Poly	----	Gorod	1961-1971	1971-

* The key to the profile categories, including an explanation of the abbreviations used, can be found on pages 9-12.

Sect. or Org.[g]	Presidium Sup. Sov.[g]	Council of Ministers[g]	Other Important Experience	Travel Outside Bloc	Why Off Politb.	Cause of Death[h]
----	Prs	Yes	----	Much	Hlth	Ntrl
Yes	Yes	----	AgP	----	Rem	----
Yes				Much	Died	Ntrl
Fst	Prs	Yes	----	Much	Died	Ntrl
----	----	Yes	Gos	Much	Rem	----
		Pm		Much	Hlth	Ntrl
Yes	Prs	----	----	Some	Rem	----
----	----	Yes	Ag Amb	Some	Rem	----
Yes	----	Yes	Ag	Some	Rem	----
Yes	----	----	----	Little	Rem?	----
Yes	----	Yes	KGB Koms	----	Hlth	----
----	----	----	Dip	Some	Rem	----
----	----	----	----	Some	Hlth	----
----	----	----	Dip Teach	Some	Rem	Ntrl
----	Yes	----	----	Much	----	----

Profile 9
THE BREZHNEV POLITBURO, 1964-1972 (Continued)

a Family Back.	b Nation-ality	Year into Party	c Higher Ed.	d Military Exp.	e Repub. or Region 1st Sec	f Years Cand. Politburo or Presidium	f Years Full Politburo or Presidium
KULAKOV, Fedor Davydovich, 1918-1978							
Wkr?	Russ	1940	Ag	----	Krai	----	1971-1978
KUNAEV, Dinmukhamed Akhmedovich, 1912-							
Int	Kazak	1939	Poly	----	Kazak	1966-1971	1971-
SHCHERDITSKY, Vladimir Vasil'evich, 1918-							
Wkr	Ukrain	1941	Poly	Cmdr	Ukrain	1961-1963 1965-1971	1971-
CANDIDATE MEMBERS ONLY DURING THE PERIOD							
ANDROPOV, Yurii Vladimirovich, 1914-1984							
Wkr?	Russ	1939	Univ	Gen	----	1966-1973	1973-1984
USTINOV, Dmitrii Fedorovich, 1908-1984							
Wkr	Russ	1927	Eng	Mshl	----	1965-1976	1976-1984
SOLOMENTSEV, Mikhail Sergeevich, 1913-							
Peas	Russ	1940	Poly	----	Oblast	1971-1983	1983-

g Sect. or Org.	g Pre-sidium Sup. Sov.	g Council of Ministers	Other Important Experience	Travel Outside Bloc	Why Off Politb.	h Cause of Death
Yes	----	Yes	Ag	----	Died	Ntrl
----	Yes	----	----	Some	----	----
----	----	Yes	----	Little	----	----
Fst	Prs	Yes	KGB	Some	Died	Ntrl
Yes	----	Yes	DfMin	Some	Died	Ntrl
Yes	----	----	Chm CPCC	Some	----	----

Table 13

COMPOSITE MEASURES OF MEANS OF POLITBURO PERIODS: 1946-72*

	1946-51	1953-56	1957-63	1964-72
Number on Politburo	11	10	13	12
The change-index	-8	+2	+16	-2
% off from				
previous year (a)	3	16	17	6
% off health reasons (b)	3	2	0	2
% new (c)	8	5	14	8
Age Frst. Sec. first year	67	59	63	58
Politburo means				
Age	55	59	59	60
Total years served (d)	13	14	7	7
Origins in %				
Peasant	64	60	55	43
Worker	30	40	45	55
Intellectual	6	0	0	2
Russian	64	75	68	55
Ukrainian	0	5	12	27
Other Nationality	36	20	20	18
Education in %				
Some higher	3	29	41	43
Polytechnical	33	16	39	54
Experience in %				
Regional Frst. Sec.	23	25	64	48
Republic Frst. Sec	17	15	19	34
Apprenticeship (e)	82	80	94	82
Secretariat	67	60	74	52
Presidium Sup. Sov.	46	30	33	25
Council of Ministers	100	91	56	47
Travel outside Bloc (f)	57	85	83	90

*Means for all of the years within each of the periods.

a-The percentage of the previous year's Politburo that is not returned, b-the percentage of the previous year's Politburo not returned for health reasons, c-the percentage of that year's Politburo that is new, d-years served at that point in time, e-previous service either as a candidate or full Politburo member, f-excluding travel prior to 1917.

Certainly, Brezhnev's years at the helm did not encompass anything like the dramatic events that occurred during Khrushchev's time in office. No serious challenge to Brezhnev's leadership surfaced midway during his term. Demographic changes on the Politburo more and more came to reflect actuarial realities, not removals from office. Beriya was the last Politburo member to be executed. No one who has exited from that body since Khrushchev has been subjected to widespread public criticism. Still, I believe that the time division made here is justifiable.

As reported in Table 8 above, the change-index for 1973 was a +20. Voronov (1961-73) and Shelest (1964-73) were removed from the Politburo in 1973. Health was not given as a reason for their dismissal. They were replaced by Andropov (1973-76), Grechko (1973-76) and Gromyko (1973-). Perhaps those who were cast out objected to the policy changes at that time. Certainly the long-time Foreign Minister Gromyko went along with the idea of detente and foreign grain purchases.

Again, I must stress that my identification of 1973 as the beginning of a sub-period is a challengeable judgement, although it is supported by the change-index measure. As far as additions to the Politburo are concerned there were actually more in 1971 (four) than in 1973 (three). The key difference is the two dismissals in 1973. This leads me to suspect that what really happened is that internal Politburo disagreements arose as early as 1971, prompting Brezhnev to add the members that he added in that year, but the climax of the disagreements was not reached until 1973, resulting in the two removals, which account for half of all of those removed by Brezhnev from 1973 through 1981. See Profile 10, "The Brezhnev Politburo: 1973-81.

Although Brezhnev's power and authority did not follow a rollercoaster path, his command of the leadership probably peaked in the early 1970s and started to decline with his failing health near the end. More importantly, the division of his era into two parts is justified primarily by the importance of the 1973 changes. Having said as much, I do not disagree with Archie Brown's analysis of the 1973 changes as moves which cannot be "solely, or even primarily," understood as actions designed to further strengthen Brezhnev's position. (2)

As Brown rightly points out, although Brezhnev came to be more than just primus inter pares, by the early 1970s, the First Secretary of the CPSU was not the all-dominant figure that Stalin, or even Khrushchev, had been. (3)

Profile 10
THE BREZHNEV POLITBURO, 1973-1981*

a Family Back.	b Nation- ality	Year into Party	c Higher Ed.	d Military Exp.	e Repub. or Region 1st Sec	f Years Cand.	f Years Full
						Politburo or Presidium	
FULL VOTING MEMBERS							
SUSLOV, Mikhail Andreevich (Reentry), 1902-1982							
Peas	Russ	1921	Ecn	Cmdr	Oblast	----	1952-1953 1955-1982
BREZHNEV, Leonid Il'ich, 1906-1982							
Wkr?	Russ	1931	Eng	LtG	Kazak	1952-1953 1956-1957	1957-1982
KOSYGIN, Aleksey Nikolaevich (Reentry), 1904-1980							
Wkr?	Russ	1927	Poly	----	----	1946-1948 1957-1960	1948-1952 1960-1980
PODGORNY, Nikolai Viktorovich, 1903-							
Wkr?	Ukrain	1930	Poly	----	Ukrain	1958-1960	1960-1977
POLYANSKY, Dmitrii Stepanivich, 1917-							
Peas	Ukrain	1939	Poly	----	Oblast	1958-1960	1960-1976
KIRILENKO, Andrei Pavlovich, 1906-							
Peas	Russ	1931	Poly	Cmdr	Oblast	1957-1961	1962-1982
SHELEPIN, Aleksandr Nikolaevich, 1918-							
Wkr?	Russ	1940	Inst	Cmdr	----	----	1964-1975
MAZUROV, Kirill Trofimovich, 1914-							
Peas	Bel	1940	Poly	Cmdr	Bel	1957-1965	1965-1978
PEL'SHE, Arvid Yanovich, 1899-1984							
Wkr?	Lat	1915	PolA	Cmdr	Lat	----	1966-1982
GRISHIN, Viktor Vasil'evich, 1914-							
Wkr	Russ	1939	Poly	----	Gorod	1961-1971	1971-
KULAKOV, Fedor Davydovich, 1918-1978							
Wkr?	Russ	1940	Ag	----	Krai	----	1971-1978
KUNAEV, Dinmukhamed Akhmedovich, 1912-							
Int	Kazak	1939	Poly	----	Kazak	1966-1971	1971-
SHCHERBITSKY, Vladimir Vasil'evich, 1918-							
Wkr	Ukrain	1941	Poly	Cmdr	Ukrain	1961-1963 1965-1971	1971-

* The key to the profile categories, including an explanation of the abbreviations used, can be found on pages 9-12.

Sect. or Org.[g]	Pre- sidium Sup. Sov.[g]	Council of Ministers[g]	Other Important Experience	Travel Outside Bloc	Why Off Politb.	Cause of Death[h]
Yes	Yes	----	AgP	----	Rem	----
Yes				Much	Died	Ntrl
Fst	Prs	Yes	----	Much	Died	Ntrl
----	----	Yes	Gos	Much	Rem	----
		Pm		Much	Hlth	Ntrl
Yes	Prs	----	----	Some	Rem	----
----	----	Yes	Ag Amb	Some	Rem	----
Yes	----	----	----	Little	Rem?	----
Yes	----	Yes	KGB Koms	----	Hlth	----
----	----	----	----	Some	Hlth	----
----	----	----	Dip Teach	Some	Rem	Ntrl
----	Yes	----	----	Much	----	----
Yes	----	Yes	Ag	----	Died	Ntrl
----	Yes	----	----	Some	----	----
----	----	Yes	----	Little	----	----

Profile 10
THE BREZHNEV POLITBURO, 1973-81 (Continued)

a Family Back.	b Nation- ality	Year into Party	c Higher Ed.	d Military Exp.	e Repub. or Region 1st Sec	f Years Cand. Politburo or Presidium	f Years Full Politburo or Presidium
ANDROPOV, Yurii Vladimirovich, 1914-1984							
Wkr?	Russ	1939	Univ	Gen	----	1966-1973	1973-1984
GRECHKO, Andrei Antonovich, 1903-1976							
Peas	Ukrain	1928	MilA	Mshl	----	----	1973-1976
GROMYKO, Andrei Andreevich, 1909-							
Peas	Russ	1931	Ecn	----	----	----	1973-
ROMANOV, Grigorii Vasil'evich, 1923-							
Peas	Russ	1944	Poly	----	Oblast	1973-1976	1976-1985
USTINOV, Dmitrii Fedrovich, 1908-1984							
Wkr	Russ	1927	Eng	Mshl	----	1965-1976	1976-1984
CHERNENKO, Konstantin Ustinovich, 1911-1985							
Peas	Russ	1931	Ped	Cmdr	Oblast	1977-1978	1978-1985
TIKHONOV, Nikolai Aleksandrovich, 1905-							
Int	Ukrain	1940	Eng	----	----	1978-1979	1979-
GORBACHEV, Mikhail Sergeevich, 1931-							
Peas	Russ	1952	Lw	----	Krai	1979-1980	1980-
CANDIDATE MEMBERS ONLY DURING THE PERIOD							
ALIEV, Geidar Alievich, 1923-							
Wkr	Azeri	1945	Hist	MjG	----	1976-1982	1982-
SOLOMENTSEV, Mikhail Sergeevich, 1913-							
Peas	Russ	1940	Poly	----	Oblast	1971-1983	1983-
KUZNETSOV, Vasilii Vasil'evich, 1901-							
Peas	Russ	1927	Eng	----	----	1944-1952 1977-1985	1952-1953
SHEVARDNADZE, Eduard Amvrosievich, 1928-							
Int	Georg	1948	Ped	Gen	Gorod	1978-1985	1985-
RASHIDOV, Sharaf Rashidovich, 1917-							
Wkr?	Uzb	1939	Ped	Cmdr	Uzb	1961-1984	----

Sect. or Org. [g]	Presidium Sup. Sov. [g]	Council of Ministers [g]	Other Important Experience	Travel Outside Bloc	Why Off Politb.	Cause of Death [h]
Fst	Prs	Yes	KGB	Some	Died	Ntrl
----	----	Yes	DfMin	Some	Died	Ntrl
----	Prs	Yes	Ag Amb Dip ForMin Prof	Much	----	----
Yes	Yes	----	FstSec Len	Much	Rem	----
Yes	----	Yes	DfMin	Some	Died	----
Fst	Prs	----	----	Much	Died	Ntrl
----	----	Pm	Gos	Much	----	----
Fst	----	----	Ag Koms	Much	----	----
----	----	Yes	NKVD KGB MVD	Some	----	----
Yes	----	----	Chm CPCC	Some	----	----
Yes	Yes	----	Amb Dip TU	Much	Rem	----
----	----	Yes	ForMin Koms MVD FstSec Georg	Some	----	----
----	----	----	Dip Teach	Much	Rem	----

Profile 10
THE BREZHNEV POLITBURO, 1973-1981 (Continued)

a Family Back.	b Nation-ality	Year into Party	c Higher Ed.	d Military Exp.	e Repub. or Region 1st Sec	f Years Cand. Politburo or Presidium	f Years Full Politburo or Presidium
DEMICHEV, Petr Nilovich, 1918-							
Wkr	Russ	1939	Eng	Cmdr	Gorod	1964-	----
MASHEROV, Petr Mironovich, 1918-1980							
Peas	Bel	1943	Pedag	Cmdr	Bel	1966-1980	----
PONAMAREV, Boris Nikolaevich, 1905-							
Int	Russ	1919	Univ	Cmdr	----	1972-	----
KISELEV, Tikhon Yakovlevich, 1917-							
Wkr?	Bel	1940	PolA	----	Bel	1980-1984	----

g Sect. or Org.	g Pre- sidium Sup. Sov.	g Council of Ministers	Other Important Experience	Travel Outside Bloc	Why Off Politb.	h Cause of Death
Yes	Yes	----	CltMin	----	----	----
----	Yes	----	Koms Teach	Some	Died	Ntrl
Yes	----	----	Hist ForAf Teach	Much	----	----
----	Yes	----	----	Some	Rem	----

The big pursuit of international policies that would bolster domestic concerns began in the early 1970s. The number of Jewish citizens allowed to emigrate increased significantly. Perhaps the most important event of all was the decision to make major purchases of foreign grain in 1972, followed by the US grain deal and similar arrangements with other major grain exporters.

Not only have the massive grain purchases been an implicit admission of the seriousness of the continuing Soviet agricultural crisis, but they also have underscored the seriousness with which the Politburo has regarded citizen welfare, or at least public opinion and what might happen if the Soviet diet were allowed to deteriorate.

Even with the massive import of grains, largely feedgrains, Soviet meat production increases per capita almost have come to a halt since the mid-1970s. Meat remains in short supply. Without the grain imports the availability of livestock produce per capita would have declined in recent years. That fact alone has had to have been a major Politburo concern since 1972.

As revealed in Table 12 above, grain production per capita rose to 773 kilograms in 1970. Since that year average annual output has been only 725 kilograms per capita. Soviet planners have long stated that fully meeting the nation's needs requires an annual output of one metric ton of grain per capita each year. The stated norm for meat consumption has varied from some 80 to 90 kilograms per capita per year (U.S. consumption is approximately 100 kgs.). However, we see that since reaching a new peak (at that time) of 59 kgs. of average annual meat produced per capita in 1975, average annual meat output per capita virtually has stagnated. Indeed, were it not for the fact that since 1975 more than 15% of all the Soviet available grain has been imported (most of which is feed grains), Soviet meat production would have fallen significantly. The point deserves repeating. In spite of enormous increases in investment in agriculture, without the massive import of grains since the early 1970s, Soviet availability of both grain and meat per capita would have declined significantly. Even with the feedgrain imports, the state stores in many cities often have no meat for sale.

Although the use of labels, like the designation of time periods, can distort understanding, it can also help further understanding. Seen from this perspective, I like best the term Valerie Bunce and John M. Echols III applied to the Brezhnev era, "corporatism politics." (4)

While I do believe that distortions have arisen from the attempt by some analysts to claim that the impact of interest groups on Soviet politics is comparable to their impact in parliamentary and congressional systems, Bunce and Echols are on the mark in asserting that important elements of corporatism have arisen in the USSR. As they state, "essentially corporatism refers to a decision-making structure in which major functional interest groups are incorporated into the policy process by the state and its leaders." (5)

In no way under Brezhnev did interest groups, the public, or the experts rise to the top, but certainly much more than ever before they were placed on tap. (6) Most importantly, a hallmark of the Brezhnev era was to keep those below the Politburo, especially the second level bureaucrats, content with their lot. Conflict at all levels was diminished, while cooperation and participation was encouraged.

Near the end of Brezhnev's rule, events in Poland and Afghanistan became disquieting, but domestically, business in the USSR became more and more calm, indeed bland. However, as one colleague rightfully stresses, "Communism makes no sense without economic growth." If the trend of recent years continues, real Soviet economic growth will cease; perhaps even a recession Soviet style will set in.

Basic to Soviet economic growth is resolving the agricultural problem. In our view no more striking, but mute, evidence for the seriousness of that problem can be found than in one of the last acts of the Brezhnev Politburo. Since 1981 Soviet grain yield and production figures have disappeared from all statistical publications. Grain production data has joined the list of top-secret information which, if published, would be viewed as seriously damaging to the system.

Table 14 adds the second Brezhnev period to our examination of the composite measures of Politburo demographic changes.

Again the change-index score for the second Brezhnev period is negative. Within the Politburo, indeed throughout the bureaucracy, business as usual while not rocking the boat was the watchword.

Some of the trends that had set in earlier continued, but no dramatic changes occurred. The level of education continued to advance as did the percentage of the members of the Politburo who came from blue collar homes.

Table 14

COMPOSITE MEASURES OF MEANS OF POLITBURO PERIODS: 1946-81*

	1946-51	53-56	57-63	64-72	73-81
Number on Politburo	11	10	13	12	15
The change-index	-8	+2	+16	-2	-4
% off from previous year (a)	3	16	17	6	7
% off health reasons (b)	3	2	0	2	4
% new (c)	8	5	14	8	6
Age Frst. Sec. first year	67	59	63	58	67
Politburo means					
Age	55	59	59	60	67
Total years served (d)	13	14	7	7	9
Origins in %					
Peasant	64	60	55	43	38
Worker	30	40	45	55	53
Intellectual	6	0	0	2	9
Russian	64	75	68	55	65
Ukrainian	0	5	12	27	16
Other Nationality	36	20	20	18	19
Education in %					
Some higher	3	29	41	43	54
Polytechnical	33	16	39	54	46
Experience in %					
Regional Frst. Sec.	23	25	64	48	37
Republic Frst. Sec	17	15	19	34	34
Apprenticeship (e)	82	80	94	82	79
Secretariat	67	60	74	52	50
Presidium Sup. Sov.	46	30	33	24	45
Council of Ministers	100	91	56	47	49
Travel outside Bloc (f)	57	85	83	90	95

*Means for all of the years within each of the periods.

a-The percentage of the previous year's Politburo that is not returned, b-the percentage of the previous year's Politburo not returned for health reasons, c-the percentage of that year's Politburo that is new, d-years served at that point in time, e-previous service either as a candidate or full Politburo member, f-excluding travel prior to 1917.

Most of all the evolution to rule by a gerontocracy had now been completed. As I shall speculate in a later section, I do not foresee a time when the Soviet Union will not be ruled by a body of men the majority of whom would be enjoying retirement in other societies.

NOTES

1. KHRUSHCHEV REMEMBERS (Trans. and Ed. by Strobe Talbott, Int. and Commentary by Edward Crankshaw), Boston: Little, Brown and Company, 1970, p. ix.

2. Archie Brown, "Political Developments: Some Conclusions and an Interpretation," in Brown Archie and Kaiser Michael (Eds.). THE SOVIET UNION SINCE THE FALL OF KHRUSHCHEV, London: The MacMillan Press Ltd., 1975, p. 239.

3. Ibid. p. 239ff.

4. Valerie Bunce and John M. Echols 111, "Soviet Politics in the Brezhnev Era: 'Pluralism' or 'Corporatism?,'" in Donald R. Kelly, (Ed.). SOVIET POLITICS IN THE BREZHNEV ERA, New York: Praeger, 1980, pp. 1-26.

5. Ibid.

6. This is a point stressed by Brown in his very perceptive analysis of events as of 1975, Op. Cit., p. 244 ff.

7

The Andropov-Chernenko Interregnum (1982–84)

> [T]he most likely prospect after Brezhnev's departure is the selection of an interim leader who during a short term of two to four years in office will fail to achieve a strong position within the oligarchy and yield to a young leader who will require several years to consolidate his power. In this case the earliest that one MAY have a strong leader is the second half of the 1980s. (1)

Why, without precedent, was first one old man and then another elevated to the position of the supreme Soviet leader?

Andropov (1973-84) was 68 when he became first secretary. Chernenko (1976-84) was 73 when given the top job. The answer to the question is implicit in what has been written above.

By the early 1980s Soviet politics had become a bland, calm, don't-rock-the-boat affair. A civil-service-like mentality had surfaced throughout a system in which virtually everybody works for the USSR Incorporated. Unless someone made major errors, or proved to be seriously unworthy, one stayed on the job and could expect to be promoted to a level beyond the peak of one's competence. A corporatist mindset extended even to the Politburo. Now it was Andropov's turn and next it was Chernenko's turn to head the Soviet corporation.

An examination of the Politburo profiles produced here will support the claim that blandness had come to mark Politburo politics. (See Profile 10 above, "The Brezhnev Politburo: 1973-81" and Profile 11, "The Andropov-Chernenko Politburo: 1982-84.")

Profile 11
THE ANDROPOV-CHERNENKO POLITBURO, 1982-1984*

a Family Back.	b Nation- ality	Year into Party	c Higher Ed.	d Military Exp.	e Repub. or Region 1st Sec	f Years Cand.	f Years Full
						Politburo or Presidium	
FULL VOTING MEMBERS							
GRISHIN, Viktor Vasil'evich, 1914-							
Wkr	Russ	1939	Poly	----	Gorord	1961-1971	1971-
KUNAEV, Dinmukhamed Akhmedovich, 1912-							
Int	Kazak	1939	Poly	----	Kazak	1966-1971	1971-
SHCHERBITSKY, Vladimir Vasil'evich, 1918-							
Wkr	Ukrain	1941	Poly	Cmdr	Ukrain	1961-1963 1965-1971	1971-
ANDROPOV, Yurii Vladimirovich, 1914-1984							
Wkr?	Russ	1939	Univ	Gen	----	1966-1973	1973-1984
GROMYKO, Andrei Andreevich, 1909-							
Peas	Russ	1931	Ecn	----	----	----	1973-
ROMANOV, Grigorii Vasil'evich, 1923-							
Peas	Russ	1944	Poly	----	Oblast	1973-1976	1976-1985
USTINOV, Dmitrii Fedoroich, 1908-1984							
Wkr	Russ	1927	Eng	Mshl	----	1965-1976	1976-1984
CHERNENKO, Konstantin Ustinovich, 1911-1985							
Peas	Russ	1931	Ped	Cmdr	Oblast	1977-1978	1978-1985
TIKHONOV, Nikolai Aleksandrovich, 1905-							
Int	Ukrain	1940	Eng	----	----	1978-1979	1979-
GORBACHEV, Mikhail Sergeevich, 1931-							
Peas	Russ	1952	Lw	----	Krai	1979-1980	1980-
ALIEV, Geidar Alievich, 1923-							
Wkr	Azeri	1945	Hist	MjG	----	1976-1982	1982-
SOLOMENTSEV, Mikhail Sergeevich, 1913-							
Peas	Russ	1940	Poly	----	Oblast	1971-1983	1983-
VOROTNIKOV, Vitalii Ivanovich, 1926-							
Wkr?	Russ	1947	Poly	----	Krai	1983-1983	1983-

* The key to the profile categories, including an explanation of the abbreviations used, can be found on pages 9-12.

g Sect. or Org.	g Pre- sidium Sup. Sov.	g Council of Ministers	Other Important Experience	Travel Outside Bloc	Why Off Politb.	h Cause of Death
----	Yes	----	----	Much	----	----
----	Yes	----	----	Some	----	----
----	----	Yes	----	Little	----	----
Fst	Prs	Yes	KGB	Some	Died	Ntrl
----	Prs	Yes	Ag Amb Dip ForMin Prof	Much	----	----
Yes	Yes	----	FstSec Len	Much	Rem	----
Yes	----	Yes	DfMin	Some	Died	Ntrl
Fst	Prs	----	----	Much	Died	Ntrl
----	----	Pm	Gos	Much	----	----
Fst	----	----	Ag Koms	Much	----	----
----	----	Yes	NKVD, KGB, MVD	Some	----	----
Yes	----	----	Chm CPCC	Some	----	----
----	----	----	Amb Pm RSFSR	Little	----	----

Profile 11
THE ANDROPOV-CHERNENKO POLITBURO, 1982-1984 (Continued)

a Family Back.	b Nation- ality	Year into Party	c Higher Ed.	d Military Exp.	e Repub. or Region 1st Sec	f Years Cand. Politburo	f Years Full or Presidium
CANDIDATE MEMBERS ONLY DURING THE PERIOD							
CHEBRIKOV, Viktor Mikhailovich, 1923-							
Wkr?	Russ	1944	Eng	Cmdr	Gorod	1983-1985	1985-
SHEVARDNADZE, Eduard Amvrosievich, 1928-							
Int	Georg	1948	Ped	Gen	Gorod	1978-1985	1985-
RASHIDOV, Sharaf Rashidovich, 1917-							
Wkr?	Uzb	1939	Ped	Cmdr	Uzb	1961-1984	----
DEMICHEV, Petr Nilovich, 1918-							
Wkr	Russ	1939	Eng	Cmdr	Gorod	1964-	----
PONAMAREV, Boris Nikolaevich, 1905-							
Innt	Russ	1919	Univ	Cmdr	----	1972-	----
KUZNETSOV, Vasilii Vasil'evich, 1901-							
Peas	Russ	1927	Eng	----	----	1944-1952 1977-1985	1952-1953
KISELEV, Tikhon Yakovlevich, 1917-							
Wkr?	Bel	1940	PolA	----	Bel	1980-1984	----
DOLGIKH, Vladimir Ivanovich, 1924-							
Int	Russ	1942	Eng	----	Krai	1982-	----

g Sect. or Org.	g Pre- sidium Sup. Sov.	g Council of Ministers	Other Important Experience	Travel Outside Bloc	Why Off Politb.	h Cause of Death
----	----	----	KGB Gen	----	----	----
----	----	Yes	ForMin Koms MVD FstSec Georg	Some	----	----
----	----	----	Dip Teach	Much	Rem	----
Yes	Yes	----	CltMin	----	----	----
Yes	----	----	Hist ForAf Teach	Much	----	----
Yes	Yes	----	Amb Dip TU	Much	Rem	----
----	Yes	----	----	Some	Rem	----
Yes	----	----	----	Some	----	----

During the period, only Kirilenko (1962-82) and Pel'she (1966-82) were removed, and both dismissals might have been primarily for health reasons. Kirilenko was 74 in 1982 and Pel'she was 83 and in ill health, and he died two years later.

Although Andropov tried to reduce incompetency, and particularly at the lowest level, lagging labor discipline, neither he nor his immediate successor had enough time in office to do more than stage a holding action.

As shown in Table 15, there was little that distinguished the Andropov-Chernenko Politburos from the two prior Brezhnev Politburos.

As the comparisons among the post-World War II Politburos reveal, with a few exceptions Poltiburo demographics were frozen between Brezhnev's rise to power in 1964 and 1985.

Perhaps the most notable change is that, along with the advancing age of that body, removal for health reasons (i.e., advanced age) has come to rival removal for reasons of political incompetence in the eyes of the first secretary. Only 2% of the resignations during the 1964-72 period were for health reasons, whereas removals for such reasons accounted for 10% of the exits in the 1982-84 period.

The Soviet political myth, indeed dogma, is that the USSR is a society of workers and peasants, and only people from such origins are suited to hold the reins of power. Nevertheless, by most usual definitions, 17% of the 1982-84 Politburo could be said not to have come from worker or peasant homes. Unless there is another revolution, that percentage surely is destined to increase in the future.

Except for the changes noted above, plus trends noted previously (e.g., the increased level of education among the members), the demographic profile of the 1982-84 Politburo most probably is the profile of Politburos for the forseeable future.

Finally, before turning to an examination of what promises to be the beginning of a Gorbachev era, beyond trends that have been identified (see "The Khrushchev Legacy" above) the following is a summary of major propositions about Politburo affairs that are supported by what has been recorded above:

1. In the struggle for Lenin's mantle Stalin had won the major battle by 1924. Certainly the war was won by 1926.

2. The numbers generated do suggest that within each of the major leadership eras there were im-

portant sub-periods, at least as far as Politburo politics is concerned.

3. Leadership interregnums are an important part of Politburo history. Thus, since 1917 there have been at least three such periods --i.e., the early part of Stalin's rule (1922-25), the confusion after Stalin's death (most of 1953) and the years of Andropov-Chernenko rule (1982-84).

4. At crucial points in Soviet history, loyalty to the first secretary can be the most important of all factors for the survival of Politburo members in office --i.e., those who lasted the longest under Stalin, Khrushchev, and Brezhnev marked themselves as being the first secretary's men.

5. When faced with a major threat, especially an external threat such as during World War II, the Politburo members are capable of drawing together and abandoning internal fighting for the duration.

6. Very possibly, Khrushchev did not lose the vote in his attempted ouster in 1957. In contrast, although undoubtedly he was disappointed by the events of 1964, he accepted the fact that he was totally outvoted the second time around.

7. Domestic problems and concerns are the primary factors that drive Politburo politics.

8. Not surprisingly, whether successful or not, major attempts to achieve Soviet reforms are signaled a few years ahead of time by high rates of turnover of the Politburo membership.

NOTES

1. Seweryn Bialer, STALIN'S SUCCESSORS: LEADERSHIP STABILITY AND CHANGE IN THE SOVIET UNION, New York: Cambridge University Press, 1980, pp. 300 & 301.

Table 15

COMPOSITE MEASURES OF MEANS OF POLITBURO PERIODS: 1946-84*

	1946-51	53-56	57-63	64-72	73-81	82-84
Number on Politburo	11	10	13	12	15	12
The change-index	-8	+2	+16	-2	-4	+1
% off from previous year (a)	3	16	17	6	7	15
% off health reasons (b)	3	2	0	2	4	10
% new (c)	8	5	14	8	6	8
Age Frst. Sec. first year	67	59	63	58	67	68
Politburo means						
Age	55	59	59	60	67	67
Total years served (d)	13	14	7	7	9	7
Origins in %						
Peasant	64	60	55	43	38	40
Worker	30	40	45	55	53	43
Intellectual	6	0	0	2	9	17
Russian	64	75	68	55	65	66
Ukrainian	0	5	12	27	16	17
Other Nationality	36	20	20	18	19	17
Education in %						
Some higher	3	29	41	43	54	54
Polytechnical	33	16	39	54	46	46
Experience in %						
Regional Frst. Sec.	23	25	64	48	37	46
Republic Frst. Sec.	17	15	19	34	34	17
Apprenticeship (e)	82	80	94	82	79	91
Secretariat	67	60	74	52	50	43
Presidium Sup. Sov.	46	30	33	24	45	49
Council of Ministers	100	91	56	47	49	46
Travel outside Bloc (f)	57	85	83	90	95	100

*Means for all of the years within each of the periods.

a-The percentage of the previous year's Politburo that is not returned, b-the percentage of the previous year's Politburo not returned for health reasons, c-the percentage of that year's Politburo that is new, d-years served at that point in time, e-previous service either as a candidate or full Politburo member, f-excluding travel prior to 1917.

PART FOUR

Gorbachev and the Future

Under Brezhnev's rule both the people and the leaders in the USSR enjoyed the most tranquil period in Soviet history. However, there were prices to be paid for the policies followed. Internationally, more ground was lost than gained. Detente fell apart and victory was not forthcoming in Afghanistan. The severe problems in Poland threatened the very foundation of the western part of the empire. Domestically, on top of all of the other unsolved problems, economic growth slowed to a near halt. All that, especially the deteriorating economic situation, accompanied by the loss of three Soviet supreme leaders within the space of four years, must have shocked Chernenko's survivors into choosing a younger man for the post of first secretary, although they must have known that the new Chairman of the Board might well shake up the corporation's calm. Even so, the experience of the last three decades assured them that at the worst some might be retired early.

8

The Dawn of a Grobachev Era? (1985–??)

Perhaps the most obvious prediction about the Gorbachev era, supported by the evolving demographics, is that, barring the unlikely, Gorbachev's term as first secretary probably will exceed that of Brezhnev's 18 years, but that Stalin's record of 30 years at the helm will go unbroken. Gorbachev is a relatively young member of the Politburo, only 54 in 1985. Moreover, the lifespan of the most recently deceased members of the Politburo reached the mid-70s. However, for Gorbachev to break Stalin's record, he would still have to hold his present post in his 85th year. Soviet actuarial reality will deny him that opportunity.

Among the most striking changes in Politburo demographics over the years has been the steady increase in the age of entry into the Politburo. That change has been paralleled by a lesser, but significant, increase in lifespans. Thus, if the average tenure in office for each member of the Politburo is calculated for each year (1917-1985) for those who have completed their terms in office, the beginning of a rising, but probably sinusoidal, curve appears. If Stalin's 36-year term is excluded from the calculations, the average tenure of the incumbents on the original Politburo was only 4.1 years. Subsequently, a gradual rise in the length of tenure occurred, peaking at 24 years during the political truce of the World War II years. Following the peak of the early and mid-1940s there was a steady decline until 1970 (the earliest date of entry of the senior incumbents on the 1985 Politburo was 1971), when the average tenure of the members of that Polituburo had fallen to 14 years. Given the fact that the lifespan of the most recently demised former members of the Politburo reached the mid-70s and the fact that death in office, or poor health in old age, increasingly has been the cause for removal from that body, and that the age of entry onto the Politburo has hovered right around 60 in recent years, one can postulate that an average tenure of 17 years in office at the beginning of the 1970s was the new post-World War II low. Indeed, actuarial and demographic realities point to a conclusion that the average tenure in office will again increase and probably will approach a new peak of some 20 years, once the ultimate disposition of the 1985 Politburo is known. Again, the average age of its members is 66, while the average age of the 1985 entrants is 60, and those who entered before 1985 already have served an average of 10 years.

Another point to be made in assessing the demographic side of the prospects for a Gorbachev era is that unless the rules of the game are drastically altered, on balance the Soviet Union is destined to be ruled by a self-perpetuating gerontocracy for the forseeable future, one occasionally salted but hardly significantly altered by the cooptation of younger men in their mid-50s. Because of the deaths of several of the older men in the last few years --Suslov (1955-82) at 80, Brezhnev (1957-82) at 76, Andropov (1973-84) at 70, and Chernenko (1978-85) at 74 at the time of death-- coincident with bringing on board several somewhat younger inductees, the average age of the 1985 Politburo receded a bit from the peak of 70 reached a few years earlier. Yet, even with the addition of four newcomers in 1985 (not so young, since their average age in 1985 was 60), the average age of the Gorbachev Politburo in its first year was 66. The names and important demographic data for the 1985 Politburo is supplied in Profile 12, "The Gorbachev Politburo: 1985."

Again, the data presented above substantiates the projection that the average age of the Politburo is destined again to rise, possibly surpassing 70 years before the end of the 1980s.

Whatever the limits biological and Soviet political realities may place on Gorbachev's freedom to maneuver, in his very first moves, Gorbachev (1980-) has shown that he is an astute practitioner of Soviet leadership politics.

Romanov (1956-85), who by most accounts was Gorbachev's chief rival for the top Soviet job, was Gorbachev's Trotsky or Malenkov. Thus, playing politics according to Soviet rules, Gorbachev ousted Romanov in 1985 and added four new pieces to his chess board, Chebrikov, Ligachev, Ryzhkov, and Shevardnadze. Their votes alone, plus Gorbachev's, account for 5 of the 13 Politburo members.

Gorbachev's leapfrogging of Ligachev and Ryzhkov to full voting membership provides another indicator that he is paving the way for important changes. That action goes against the trend. Apprenticeship on that body has become increasingly important for the achievement of full voting status since the end of the Stalin Era. Even if one excludes the first two years of Bolshevik rule (1917 and 1918), because the first candidate member was not appointed until 1919, and the extraordinary year of 1952, from the calculations, only 69% of those who reached full membership between 1919 and 1952 had served an apprenticeship of either being a previous full member or a candidate member. However, among those who reached full status 1953 through 1984 75% had such apprenticeship.

Surely, the two old men of the 1985 Politburo effectively have been neutered, if not captured, by their age, their lofty postions, the politician's desire to highlight positively the pages of history, and what occurred during Gorbachev's early months in office.

Gromyko, at 76, was rewarded for his long and faithful service by being elevated to President of the Presidium of the Supreme Soviet. Technically he is now the Soviet President, entitled to twenty-one gun salutes and all of the other perquisites of a Soviet chief of state. Moreover, in his new position he still will be able to play the role of the dean of the Soviet diplomatic corps, even though the new Foreign Minister, Shevardnadze, probably is now in command of day-to-day Soviet foreign affairs.

The other old man is Tikhonov, the Chairman of the Soviet Council of Ministers, the third most important Soviet office. He reached 80 in 1985 and, barring the ravages of senility, is unlikely to want to rock the boat. (1)

If Gorbachev is patient, in a very few years either, or both, of the elderly men will be gone. The majority of the appointees clearly will be his patrons, and he can expect to emerge as powerful as any Soviet leader since Stalin.

Before turning to other matters, speculation on why Gorbachev selected Shevardnadze, who is almost totally inexperienced in foreign affairs, to be the new Foreign Minister seems in order. The most obvious answer would be that since he clearly is both inexperienced and beholden to Gorbachev for his high positions, Shevardnadze can be expected to turn to Gorbachev for advice and guidance much more than someone without such constraints. In sum, I anticipate that, even more than his predecessors, Gorbachev intends to lead in foreign policy matters.

Profile 12
THE GORBACHEV POLITBURO, 1985*

a Family Back.	b Nationality	Year into Party	c Higher Ed.	d Military Exp.	e Repub. or Region 1st Sec	f Years Cand.	f Years Full
						Politburo or Presidium	
FULL VOTING MEMBERS							
GRISHIN, Viktor Vasil'evich, 1914-							
Wkr	Russ	1939	Poly	----	Gorod	1961-1971	1971-
KUNAEV, Dinmukhamed Akhmedovich, 1912-							
Int	Kazak	1939	Poly	----	Kazak	1966-1971	1971-
SHCHERBITSKY, Vladimir Vasil'evich, 1918-							
Wkr	Ukrain	1941	Poly	Cmdr	Ukrain	1961-1963 1965-1971	1971-
GROMYKO, Andrei Andreevich, 1909-							
Peas	Russ	1931	Ecn	----	----	----	1973-
TIKHONOV, Nikolai Aleksandrovich, 1905-							
Int	Ukrain	1940	Eng	----	----	1978-1979	1979-
GORBACHEV, Mikhail Sergeevich, 1931-							
Peas	Russ	1952	Lw	----	Krai	1979-1980	1980-
ALIEV, Geidar Alievich, 1923-							
Wkr	Azeri	1945	Hist	MjG	----	1976-1982	1982-
SOLOMENTSEV, Mikhail Sergeevich, 1913-							
Peas	Russ	1940	Poly	----	Oblast	1971-1983	1983-
VOROTNIKOV, Vitalii Ivanovich, 1926-							
Wkr?	Russ	1947	Poly	----	Krai	1983-1983	1983-
CHEBRIKOV, Viktor Mikhailovich, 1923-							
Wkr?	Russ	1944	Eng	Cmdr	Gorod	1983-1985	1985-
LIGACHEV, Egor Kuz'mich, 1920-							
Wkr	Russ	1944	Poly	----	Obkom	----	1985-
RYZHKOV, Nikolai Ivanovich, 1929-							
Wkr	Russ?	1956	Eng	----	----	----	1985-
SHEVARDNADZE, Eduard Amvrosievich, 1928-							
Int	Georg	1948	Ped	Gen	Gorod	1978-1985	1985-

* The key to the profile categories, including an explanation of the abbreviations used, can be found on pages 9-12.

g Sect. or Org.	g Presidium Sup. Sov.	g Council of Ministers	Other Important Experience	Travel Outside Bloc	Why Off Politb.	h Cause of Death
----	Yes	----	----	Much	----	----
----	Yes	----	----	Some	----	----
----	----	Yes	----	Little	----	----
----	Prs	Yes	Ag Amb Dip ForMin Prof	Much	----	----
----	----	Pm	Gos	Much	----	----
Fst	----	----	Ag Koms	Much	----	----
----	----	Yes	NKVD KGB MVD	Some	----	----
Yes	----	----	Chm CPCC	Some	----	----
----	----	----	Amb Pm RSFSR	Little	----	----
----	----	----	KGB Gen	----	----	----
Yes	----	----	POrg ForAf	Some	----	----
Yes	----	Pm	----	Little	----	----
----	----	Yes	ForMin Koms MVD FstSec Georg	Some	----	----

Profile 12
THE GORBACHEV POLITBURO, 1985 (Continued)

a Family Back.	b Nation-ality	Year into Party	c Higher Ed.	d Military Exp.	e Repub. or Region 1st Sec	f Years Cand. Politburo or Presidium	f Years Full Politburo or Presidium
CANDIDATE MEMBERS ONLY DURING THE YEAR							
DEMICHEV, Petr Nilovich, 1918-							
Wkr	Russ	1939	Eng	Cmdr	Gorod	1964-	----
PONAMAREV, Boris Nikolaevich, 1905-							
Int	Russ	1919	Univ	Cmdr	----	1972-	----
DOLGIKH, Vladimir Ivanovich, 1924-							
Int	Russ	1942	Eng	----	Krai	1982-	----
SOKOLOV, Sergei Leonidovich, 1911-							
Int	Russ	1937	MilA	Cmdr Mshl	----	1985-	----
TALYZIN, Nikolai Vladimirovich, 1929-							
Wkr	Russ	1960	Eng	----	----	1985-	----

g Sect. or Org.	g Pre- sidium Sup. Sov.	g Council of Ministers	Other Important Experience	Travel Outside Bloc	Why Off Politb.	h Cause of Death
Yes	Yes	----	CltMin	----	----	----
Yes	----	----	Hist ForAf Teach	Much	----	----
Yes	----	----	----	Some	----	----
----	----	Yes	DfMin	Much	----	----
----	----	Yes	CommMin	----	----	----

Certainly, the demographic changes made by Gorbachev at the time of this writing resemble less the relatively easy transition from Khrushchev to Brezhnev and more the substantial personnel changes made by Stalin in 1926 and Khrushchev in 1952-53 and 1957. However, as of the end of 1985, Gorbachev still does not have a strong majority of his own men in the Politburo. Therefore, our speculation is that whatever major changes Gorbachev may have in mind will not begin to surface until toward the end of the 1980s, when he should have his strong majority. What might they be? That question will be a major subject of our speculation later in this analysis.

I am not the first to note that a primary career asset for achieving full membership on the Politburo is to have served successfully as a regional party boss --i.e., as a gorod, krai, or oblast first secretary. In recent years, this seems to be even more the case. Thus, whereas from 1917 to 1985, 39 percent of the Politburo incumbents had, or have had, such experience prior to achieving full Politburo status, nine of the eleven (82%) inducted since 1973 had such prior experience. True, only eight of the 13 member 1985 Politburo (62%) have had previous experience as regional first secretaries. However, that probably is an anomaly. Neither of the two most elderly members, discussed above, have held such posts, and the trend leads one to speculate that when Gromyko and Tikhonov are gone, one or both will be replaced by men who successfully have held key regional posts in their advancing careers.

Pereniallly, alcoholism, labor inefficiency, and, especially, the nationality and agricultural production problems monopolize the concerns of the Politburo. The battle against drunkenness and low worker output have continued to receive attention but, given the deep-seated causes of those two problems, the likelihood of any genuinely innovative solutions for them seems small.

As in many cultures, heavy drinking sometimes is done in celebration. However, often it is associated with life's frustrations, and many of the sources of frustration in the USSR (e.g., the overwhelmingly stifling nature of the Soviet bureaucracy in one of the most bureaucratized system in the world) seem almost impermeable to change, even by the Politburo.

Reducing the hours that the spirit shops are open and increasing prices by 25% may have some effect, including stimulating the production of illegal liquor, but superficial moves are unlikely to solve the Soviet alcohol problem.

Improving worker incentives by unleashing "Leninist profit" was the centerpiece of the "Liberman reforms" which dominated so much of the press at the height of Khrushchev's power. Nothing, but nothing, of import ever came out of the reams of paper devoted to the discussion. Nevertheless, the introduction of some of the ideas discussed during the Liberman debate may be attempted.

The nationality problem continues to be as serious as always. Yet, as long as the USSR is ruled by Russians who impose their brand of Marxist-Leninist-Stalinism on the entire empire, the emphasis will surely continue to vacillate, as it has in recent years, between Sovietization and Russification whereby greater social homogeneity and ethnic peace are pursued. Again, Politburo demographics tell an important part of the story.

Four of the seven-man original Politburo were ethnic Russians (57%). For the whole period 1917-85, sixty-two of the eighty-nine incumbents (70%) have been Russians. As of 1985 only sixty-two percent of the Gorbachev Politburo (including himself) are Russians. That percentage probably is too low and the error will be rectified in future years. Indeed, three of his four 1985 appointees were Russians.

Politburo history suggests that when Gorbachev reaches the peak of his power, he will initiate new schemes to "solve" the drinking, labor efficiency and nationality problems. But that same history bears out a prognosis that whatever is done will be merely tinkering and that little or no change and certainly no ultimate solutions will be effected.

Surely, near the top of the agenda of the Gorbachev Politburo's concerns will be the slowing rate of economic growth, including the continuing debate over the future of Soviet technology. As ably documented by Bruce Parrott, central to the discussion will be the rivalry between the "traditionalists" and the "non-traditionalists."

Hauntingly, the present-day rivalry is an echo of the Slavophile-Westernizer debate under the Tsars. Soviet scientists produced their own nuclear device. Aided by "their own" German rocket experts, the USSR was first in space. But, as Parrott documents, the "non-traditionalists" insist that technology transfer from the West is essential to future Soviet growth. Thus, in recent decades the U.S. moon landings, the continued growth of Western economies, the shock of the Prague spring, and the fact that Soviet economic growth is at a historic low and probably will slow even further are increasing apprehension among the men in the Kremlin. (2)

A survey of the Soviet press in 1984 and 1985 reveals that Soviet backwardness in the realm of computers is a key element of the debate. Computers must be more widely available. Soviet youth must be trained to use computers. But almost no reading between the lines is needed to discover a grave concern over what might happen if computers are as readily available to Soviet citizens as they are to citizens in the West. Computers allow the creation of unofficial data bases. Computers are used as word processors with individual printers.

The modern computer age is totally incompatible with a closed society where such information as national grain yield statistics are kept secret.

What might be attempted in the agricultural realm may well be the most dramatic and far reaching. I submit the fact that Gorbachev, like both Brezhnev and Khrushchev, the two previously relatively young Politburo members to win the top post since Stalin, has his political roots in that most serious domestic economic problem, agriculture, is more than coincidence.

Brezhnev, who had served as the First Secretary of Kazakhstan, took most of the credit for the "successes" of the "new lands" venture. Plowing up the "virgin lands" of Kazakhstan and the Southern RSFSR stemmed from a Politburo decision that dramatically altered the Soviet agricultural scene.

As discussed below, most ironically, Khrushchev won a Politburo battle against introducing the ZVENO form of organizing farm work and remuneration in 1952, which must have been crucial to his promotion to first secretary the following year, that was diametrically counter to a major battle won by Gorbachev in 1983, which, too, must have been crucial to his subsequent rise in power. Even more ironically, by the early 1960s, apparently Khrushchev had done an about-face and would have promoted rural changes that would have favored the ZVENO, if he had been allowed to retain his post.

No Western analyst to our knowledge (this writer included) entertained any thought that the 1983 appointment of Gorbachev to full voting membership on the Politburo was portent to his rise to supreme Soviet political post only two years later. Yet, a review of the changing Politburo dynamics of 1983 in light of past history, Politburo concerns, and Gorbachev's career reveals clues to what actually occurred.

Gorbachev is peasant in origin. He has a degree in law from Moscow State University (1955). Subsequently, he completed a correspondence course at the Stavropol Agricultural Institute in 1967. Key to his advancing career was his term as the CPSU organizer of production administration of collective and state farms in the Stavropol Kraikom (1962-63), followed later by his elevation to the post of first secretary of the Stavropol Gorkom (1966-68), and then for the whole Kraikom (1970-78). His service resulted in his being called first to the CPSU Secretariat (1978-79) as the top Party official responsible for agricultural affairs and then, in 1979, to the position of candidate member of the Politburo (1979-80).

The final clue to what the future might hold for Gorbachev came in 1983. The freshman Politburo member Gorbachev persuaded the full Politburo to endorse publicly the KOLLEKTIVNYI PODRYAD (collective contract) scheme for organizing the work and accounting on the farms.

In 1952, as now, Soviet agriculture was in serious trouble. Andreev (1934-52) had been the post-war agricultural point man for Stalin's Politburo in his waning years. During the war, since all effort was concentrated on winning against the Germans, control over the kolkhozy was largely neglected. As a result, for the only time in Soviet collective farm history, "kolkhoz democracy" had some real meaning. Instead of being appointed, for all intents and purposes, from outside by higher party authorities, kolkhoz chairmen were selected from within the farms. Most importantly to our narrative, many of the farms were, in effect, broken up into smaller, largely family enterprises. These were the ZVENO that were to cost Andreev his career.

On those farms where the ZVENO came to predominate, the work, and ofttimes the land, was broken up into smaller units. ZVENO in Russian means link or team. Thus, the responsibilty for cultivating the smaller units fell to the small teams, constituting a half-dozen or so indivduals, often from the same family.

Unlike Stalin and most of his other colleagues, Andreev often visited the countryside, and what he saw he reported and promoted in speeches. He saw the ZVENO as a success, indeed embodying the model for the future of Soviet agriculture. Challenging the large brigade system that had been imposed upon the farms as the superior Marxist-Leninist form of organizing labor --i.e., reaping the advantages of "the collective power of the masses"-- Andreev reported that the ZVENO were superior by most economic measures. Most important of all, as he and his supporters were to claim, in the grain-short USSR, yields achieved on ZVENO cultivated fields were far greater than those on farms where the brigade system had remained untouched.

Unfortunately, the wholesale adoption of the ZVENO system would have meant a serious loss of central control over agriculture. Essential to the success of the teams was that their members were freed to make their own production decisions. Not only were the "permanent" brigades rigidly controlled within the farms, but they facilitated the tight outside controls of the farms that had been imposed upon them by the Party controlled Machine-Tractor Stations which, among other things, owned all of the available machinery without which most of the crucial field work, especially at planting and harvest time, could not be accomplished.

As indicated above, the earlier ZVENO debate spread over several years, and although he was to remain on the Politburo until 1952, Andreev lost his first major battle in 1950, a revealing incident in the workings of Politburo politics. Advocating universal adoption of the system, even on the relatively more mechanized large grain farms, Andreev became a special target for his critics. Indeed, as a result of losing the argument, in a quite extraordinary exercise of SAMOKRITIKA (public self-criticism) for a full member of the Politburo, he responded, in part, as follows to a PRAVDA criticism of his position:

> Since the publication in PRAVDA of the article "Against Distortions in Kolkhoz Labor Organization," I have reflected a great deal, and must frankly acknowledge the correctness of the Bolshevik criticism of my statements on the organization of labor and the organization of links in kolkhoz grain cultivation. (3)

As the ZVENO critics were to proclaim, adoption of the system would be "a throwback to private-property instincts [that] ...represent a falacious nonsocialist path." (4) Khrushchev, however, came to the rescue of the struggle to build communism in the countryside. Not only did he join the critics of the ZVENO, but the bait he offered the peasants to turn away from the teams was his famed AGROGOROD scheme, which was to catch Stalin's, and the rest of the Politburo's attention. Essential to the idea was to build agricultural cities (AGROGORODY) in the countryside, which would provide all the amenities of city life for the peasants. How? In contrast to breaking the farms up into smaller units, if built, the AGROGORODY must have as their base huge farms, much larger than the already large collectives. Thus, a drive to amalgamate neighboring collectives was initiated and completed under Khrushchev. Today's farms are nearly ten times larger than the pre-1952 farms. That reality allowed the Party fully to penetrate the kolkhozy, making the MTS redundant instruments of central control, and Khrushchev presided over their abandonment in 1958. (5)

The AGROGORODY were never built. Although never directly admitted, clearly the key reason why the rural cities scheme was abandoned was a realization on the part of the Politburo that their successful construction would have required huge, largely non-productive, investments. Having to make choices, Soviet decison makers always have given low priority to the quality of rural housing, public libraries, centers for recreation, and other such niceties that can enhance the quality of rural life.

Before turning to Gorbachev's endorsement of the ZVENO scheme we need to elaborate upon Khrushchev's apparent about-face on the matter in the early 1960s, understanding that change not only further illuminates Khrushchev's policy and problems during his final years in office, but it underscores the difficulties faced by Gorbachev if he is bent upon achieving major agricultural reform.

Alexander Yanov's eyewitness account of Khrushchev's lost reform is a penetrating revelation of the obstacles faced by Khrushchev in the 1960s and by Gorbachev in the 1980s.

Neither this researcher nor Yanov has been able to find a word of direct praise for the ZVENO by Khrushchev. However, Yanov convincingly argues that the adoption of the ZVENO scheme would have been a logical outgrowth of the rural reforms attempted by Khrushchev in the early 1960s. As noted by Yanov, Khrushchev did support his move against the rural prefects by proclaiming that: "'The facelessness of the earth must be terminated; the field must have its master.'" (6) As noted earlier, Khrushchev's immediate target was the rural prefects and, as a result, in 1960-61 alone "more-than-half" of the rayon first secretaries in the Russian and Ukrainian republics were dismissed. (7)

Still, I must admit that what Khrushchev thought about the ZVENO at that time is far from clear. The Khrushchev "the field must have its master" statement was in issue No. 4 of OKTIABR," 1961. Yet, as late as February, 1960, Khrushchev referred to the ZVENO advocates by stating that they "had pulled the kolkhozy back and led them into a weakened position." (8) Of course, he was quite capable of changing his mind, and may well have done so within the year.

Unfortunately, for both Khrushchev and the ill-fated reform, as noted in our earlier discussion, the prefects and their supporters were galvanized into action and were to play an important role in Khrushchev's downfall in 1964. Further, the lesson was not lost on Brezhnev. Consistent with his attitude of "if you can't defeat the opposition join them," he supported the rural prefects. Yanov poses the question, what was behind Brezhnev's move to pour unprecedented amounts of capital into the farms? Of course, he hoped to solve the food problem, but Yanov believes that a major motive was "a bribe paid to provincial elites," designed "TO ELIMINATE THE LINK ALTERNATIVE." (9)

In essence the March 1983 Politburo endorsement of the collective contract scheme, upon Gorbachev's urgings, was a resounding victory for the pro-ZVENO forces in a battle that has waxed and waned since Khrushchev's victory over Andreev in 1952. The ZVENO were never stomped out completely and, obviously, Gorbachev came to appreciate them as a means of increasing peasant incentives, and therefore productivity, while saving on expenses. Although the provisions for contracting the work to smaller (often family) groups of workers carry some new twists, the scheme retains the essential ingredients of the old idea. Moreover, and quite astoundingly, an IZVESTIA contributor made the following observation about the new system in 1983: "Each hectare will get a proprietor, and signposts will appear across our land: "'S. S. Zhelebrovsky's Land,' 'V. I. Bolotov's Land,' 'V. Ye. Rashchupkon's Land' and 'A. F. Uvarov's Land.'" (10) Practicing "goulash communism," Hungary has greatly freed its farmers. A counter-revolution of enormous proportions has accompanied the introduction of the "responsibility principle" into the Chinese countryside. In 1983 Gorbachev opened the doors of the Kremlin just enough for his colleagues to consider similar sweeping changes in the USSR. But, in contemplating the implications of fully adopting of the new scheme, Gorbachev and his colleagues have probably come to realize that, fully implemented, the collective contracts would pose a fundamental threat to the Stalinist system and, thus, their high positions.

In 1983 and 1984 the Soviet press was full of praises of the collective contract system. Apparently, roughly half of the farms, at least in name, went over to the new scheme in the early months. Although not a single word of criticism of the idea has appeared in print, Gorbachev and others often have admitted that there are some potholes in the road to change in the countryside. Moreover, only rarely is there mention of the scheme in the 1985 press. Gorbachev, although now the First Secretary of the CPSU, has not yet breathed new life into the discussion. Why? Surely the contract system is attractive in that its proponents claim that it would boost production and at the same time reduce costs.

Not all of the farms that changed over to the new system have stayed with it. The experience of one wealthy Western Siberia state farm that converted to the new system, and then abandoned it, probably provides one reason why, as of 1985, the scheme seems dead in the water. On that farm, a contract team of machine operators disbanded when their earnings had doubled. They said the reason was that there was nothing in the local shops that they wanted to spend their increased earnings on. Why should they work harder to earn more money to buy things that weren't available? As the IZVESTIA reporter who wrote the story concluded: "The organization of teams, with their opportunities for increased earnings, should be accompanied by growth in the supply of goods and services in rural localities." (11)

Reaping fully the benefits of the collective contract system clearly requires changes beyond the boundaries of the farms. Undoubtedly, Gorbachev and his colleagues at least suspect that decontrolling prices and opening up a free market are logical next steps that might break the economic logjam stifling both agricultural and industrial worker initiative. But changes in that direction not only are retrogressive from building communism, but, most important of all, such changes must be paid for in substantial losses of central, specifically, Politburo, controls over the economy and the citizenry. As one Soviet journalist wrote: "The contract system is unthinkable without high overall standards in economic thinking at all levels of the country's economy --from the central planning organs to ...the accounting clerk at a collective or state farm." (12)

Yet the imperative for change continues to mount. Since 1972 the USSR has been dependent upon massive, and costly, grain imports. In 1978, the USSR harvested an all-time record grain crop, a year when the weather may have been the best ever. Subsequently, all the harvests (1979-85) have been disappointing, far below plan, and as Gorbachev has implied, far below that needed to sustain the quality of diet (especially livestock products) demanded by Soviet citizens.

Brezhnev presided over massive increases in investment in agriculture. But even before he died, it became apparent that a point of diminishing returns had been reached. Clearly, just throwing more rubles at the farms was not enough to solve the Soviet agricultural problem.

What is to be done?

At the time of this writing, late 1985, Gorbachev's most important pronouncements on the agricultural problem were made in a speech to a conference of Party workers in Tselinograd (the center of the Kazakh new lands area) on September 7, 1985. What he did and did not say on that occasion fits with the above.

INTENTSIFIKATSIA was his major theme. There are no more new lands to put to plow. Future increases in food production must come from increased yields on improved lands (e.g., irrigated or drained land) and improved productivity on those lands not subject to reclamation. In his speech he admitted:

> [O]ur per capita consumption of meat and fruit is lower than in some countries and is somewhat below the established national norms of nutrition...

[M]eat production is an element of the greatest strain... We are lagging behind in this field.... Demand for some.... [foodstuffs] exceeds their supply.

....

[O]ur shops sell meat at prices which make up one-third or a half of its prime cost.... [T]he state subsidy... amounts to an impressive 20,000 million roubles a year in the case of meat.

....

Failures in meeting the plans for the production and purchase of grain cause tension in the adequate satisfaction of the country's needs. This forces us to import grain and to spend sizable hard-currency reserves for this purpose. [No previous Soviet leader has noted this reality in public.]

....

[T]he paramount issue... is the observance of technological discipline in the fields... [T]he potential of scientific farming systems is still being inadequately used in many places. (13)

The above is very important, but there were two other salient messages buried in his speech, and they are closely related. At one point, he changed the subject from that of criticism of past failures and stated: "Everything depends here on the activity of leading cadres, Party, government and economic bodies, AND NOT ON ADDITIONAL CAPITAL INVESTMENTS. [This writer's italics.] (14)

If Gorbachev has his way, the Brezhnev approach to the food problem is finished. There will be no more "bribes" (Yanov) for the rural prefects. Leadership, organizational and economic reforms which do not cost billions of new investments must provide the solution to Soviet agriculture's problems, if there is to be a solution.

Only once in his speech, for the first time since he has been first secretary, did he refer to the contract (thus ZVENO) system. Fairly early in his address he stated: "The introduction of the cost-accounting and team contract scheme has a favorable influence on people's attitude to work and on the results of their work." Soviet leaders and citizens, trained to look for the whole message, will not fail to connect his favorable references to the team contract scheme (given his 1983 promotion of their universal adoption) to his remarks at the very close of the speech:

> What is required is an enterprising effort in the nation's agrarian sector.... I would like to refer in this context to the role of our rural district Party committees. There are 3,200 of them now. They are in charge of over 49,000 collective and state farms.... [H]owever, ...many district Party committees are slow in reorganizing their work and sometimes forget that a Party committee is a political governing body.... Some district committees stray off to an improper style. It is sometimes difficult to distinguish the forms and methods of the work of a Party committee from those of an economic body. (15)

The above, of course, was the essence of Khrushchev's criticisms when he attempted his ill-fated agricultural reforms of the early 1960s. Surely, his failure contributed to his removal in 1964.

The USSR is faced with a new "time of troubles." Fundamental change is called for. When Gorbachev approaches, or reaches, the peak of his power and authority, he may ask the Politburo to sanction the most sweeping internal changes in the USSR in decades, perhaps ever. However, the obstacles to achieving such changes are enormous. They will be the major concern in my concluding observations.

NOTES

1. At the time of this writing press accounts state that Tikhonov has stepped down from the position of Chairman of the Council of Ministers, replaced by Ryzhkov (1985-). However, there is no account of his having retired from the Politburo.

2. Bruce Parrott, POLITICS AND TECHNOLOGY IN THE SOVIET UNION, Cambridge, Massachusetts: The MIT Press, 1983, p. 331 ff.

3. See A. Andreev, "V pobody staty, opyvlikovannoi v gazete PRAVDA 19.II.50g. 'Protiv izvrashchenii v organizatsii truda v kolkhozakh," PRAVDA, February 28, 1950, p. 4.

4. A. Strelyany, KOMSOMOLSKAYA PRAVDA, October 15, 1965.

5. Roy D. Laird, Darwin E. Sharp and Ruth Sturtevant, THE RISE AND FALL OF THE MTS AS AN INSTRUMENT OF SOVIET RULE, Lawrence, Kansas: The University of Kansas Publications, Governmental Research Series No. 22, 1960.

6. Alexander Yanov, THE DRAMA OF THE SOVIET 1960S: A LOST REFORM, Berkeley: University of California Institute of International Studies, 1984, p. 60.

7. Ibid. p. 73.

8. PRAVDA, February 19, 1960, pp. 2-5.

9. Yanov, Op. Cit., p. 115.

10. Leonid Shinkarev, IZVESTIA, March 28, 1983, p. 2.

11. Leonid Shinkarev, "One's Own Land," IZVESTIA, March 17, 1983, p. 2.

12. Lev Voskrensky, "From Piece Work to Contract," MOSCOW NEWS, Nos. 14 & 15, 1983.

13. Michail Gorbachev "Secure Intensive Growth of Farming and Related Industries," PRAVDA, September 11, 1985.

14. Ibid.

15. Ibid.

9

A New "Time of Troubles"

> [I]t is on the one hand impossible to continue present policy, and on the other equally impossible to undertake change.... WITHIN the given system there is no solution to the crisis. (1)
>
> ....
>
> Soviet economists and virtually all Western specialists would agree that small-scale tinkering can no longer sufffice and that the question "What is to be done?" concerns the change from guidance based on ADMINISTRATIVE ORDERS to that based on ECONOMIC PARAMETERS. (2)

Is the Politburo leadership system, designed by Lenin and Stalin in the first quarter of the century, suited to alleviate the serious problems faced by the Soviet Union in the 1980s?

In many ways the Politburo is the most powerful political body in the world. As stressed above, the bureaucracy is the base upon which most of the Politburo's power rests. Yet, the bureaucracy also seriously limits that power, and thus can be seen as at the root of a new "time of troubles" that must be faced by the men in the Kremlin. (3)

Of course, the upheaval of the thirties and, especially, the German invasion during World War II were far greater threats to the USSR than the problems faced today. Yet, reading both on the lines and between the lines of the Soviet press, Western observers are not alone in the judgement that the USSR is in a new crisis period, with problems of a whole new dimension that largely are manifested in a faltering economy. Indeed, on the lines, Gorbachev has stated that the situation demands "transformations of a truly historic scale." (4)

Although no alarm as such has been sounded, Gorbachev's remarks and the content of the "draft" new "Program of the Communist Party of the Soviet Union" make the point that fundamental reform is called for. Thus in his October 1985 "Report" to the CPSU Central Committee Gorbachev stressed that "the Program proceeds from the decisive role of the economy in society's development..., aimed at transformations on a truly historic scale --accomplishment of a new technical remodeling of the economy, transferring it to an intensive path of development,..." Further, and most revealing he stated: "It is worthy of note that in the new Five-Year Plan growth in national income and output of all branches of material production will be achieved entirely, for the first time, by raising productivity. (5)

As noted here previously, earlier in 1985 in his major agricultural speech at Tselenograd, Gorbachev stated that increased food production could not come from new investments, that increased productivity must come from improved efficiency on the existing base. Now he is saying that the same applies for the whole economy. Why? Apparently the leadership has come to realize that there are few, if any, rubles left for increased investment. Most importantly, they have recognized what many Western critics long have stressed. The mounting inefficiencies of the centrally planned command system, dominated by an intransigent bureaucracy, have brought the Soviet economy to a point of stagnation. What worked at a time when labor and, especially, untapped natural resources were abundant will not work today.

The draft Party program spells it all out in italics. Success is to be achieved by:

> A NEW TECHNICAL RECONSTRUCTION OF THE NATIONAL ECONOMY..., RENEWAL OF THE PRODUCTION APPARATUS ON A BASIS OF ADVANCED TECHNOLOGY..., INCREASE IN LABOR PRODUCTIVITY..., improvement in UTILIZATION OF NATURAL ENERGY RESOURCES, RAW AND OTHER MATERIALS, FUEL AND ENERGY..., [and] ON BETTER USE OF FIXED ASSETS. [Moreover,] switching to intensive national economic growth calls for serious STRUCTURAL CHANGES. (6)

As Gorbachev noted in his "Report," in framing the draft, the Party "encountered problems of a different kind, ones stemming from the fact that not all of our cadres have given up inertia, old patterns and adherence to extensive methods of economic management." (7) Although clothed in the usual rhetoric, the new program is calling for major, fundamental change, improvements that cannot be bought by rubles at any price. Old administrative ways and existing mindsets just will not do.

Yet, how much change will the massive Soviet bureaucracy accept? Indeed, how much change is the Politburo itself willing to push?

When compared to other top leadership groups (e.g., a British or U.S. cabinet or, even, the PRC Politburo), the Soviet Politburo stands out as one of the most conservative political bodies in the world. Why? I submit that the answer can be found in Soviet history, including that of the evolving Politburo itself.

FIRST: THE RULES OF SOVIET LEADERSHIP POLITICS, INCLUDING THE MECHANICS OF POLITBURO MEMBERSHIP, CONTRIBUTE CONSIDERABLY TO THE ULTRACONSERVATIVE NATURE OF THE POLITBURO.

As compared to most nations, certainly the parliamentary democracies, the average tenure in office of the top Soviet political leadership is quite long, several times that of a British, French or U.S. cabinet member. Thus, the same old men with the same old ideas stay on and on. Moreover, when they do step down, or are removed, their successors inevitably come from the same mold, never from an opposition party that has won a recent election based upon a promise to throw the rascals out and initiate new policies. Political opposition, even in-Party factionalism, is illegal. Indeed, it is viewed as evil in the USSR.

Far more than the top political leaders in most other societies, especially those with parliamentary-congressional systems, the top Soviet leadership is establishment oriented. In George Simmonds' words: "There is a remarkable similarity in the background, careers, and outlook of the chief leaders of the Soviet party and government." (8)

As powerful as the first secretary of the CPSU may be, the claim that since Stalin, Politburo decisions have been led by "collective leadership" is not entirely meaningless. In the USSR, whatever public criticism is voiced against top political figures, it is reserved for the fallen, and always directed against their failure to conform to the Politburo's current line. According to our count, between 1917 and 1985, of the 89 incumbents who have served on the Politburo, 53 (60%) have been expelled or removed from that body. What was their major fault? They had unacceptable new ideas and/or they were in opposition to their colleagues.

Although post-removal disgrace is not as severe as it once was, almost none of those removed have escaped from being held up to public ridicule. Of course, some former

Western public officials (including former US presidents) are ridiculed, but rarely to the extent that are former Politburo members. The contrast between the fate of Nixon and that of Khrushchev is illustrative of the point. Whether for health reasons or not, Khrushchev was forced to resign, condemned for his errors, banished to his country dacha and totally cut off from public exposure. His memoirs were not published in the USSR. Nixon, while condemned and forced to resign his office, is still free to speak, write and move about like any other citizen. Many, including those in high government places, still seek Nixon's advice.

If one's only knowledge of Soviet political history depended upon post-1964 Soviet publications, one would never know that for more than a decade Khrushchev was the most powerful man in the USSR. At best, the Soviet press occasionally records his existence in the obscurity of a footnote. In the official history, SOVIET FOREIGN POLICY: VOLUME II: 1945-1980, edited by Politburo member A. A. Gromyko and candidate Politburo member B. N. Ponomarev, 221 pages are devoted to the years when Khrushchev was at the Soviet helm. (9) At most his name is mentioned a half dozen times --i.e., where it would be totally ludicrous to omit the fact that he had existed. There is complete silence about his accession of power, no hint that there was a Malenkov interregnum, or that the idea of peaceful coexistence (which receives much space) was first pushed under Khrushchev. Moreover, if one were to rely only on the Gromyko-Ponomarev volume, one would never know that there was a Khrushchev de-Stalinization speech, which was to have such a profound impact upon Soviet international relations, especially within the Eastern European part of the empire and with the PRC.

Not just history, but how the men in the Kremlin interpret history in their relationships with one another, is essential to understanding Politburo affairs, including its members' reluctance to effect change.

SECOND: THE USE OF THE MARXIST-LENINIST "SCIENCE OF SOCIETY" AS THE ULTIMATE SOURCE OF LEGITIMACY FOR BOTH THE SYSTEM AND THE LEADERSHIP PLACES IMPORTANT CONSTRAINTS ON POLITBURO INITIATIVE. Here, the contrast with the experience of the PRC is both striking and illuminating. Although both systems inaugurated major changes after the passing of their two founders, Lenin and Mao, the post-Mao changes in China to date are much more profound than the Soviet changes in the whole post-Stalin period. I think one key to the difference lies in Stalin's success in deifying Lenin. In contrast, Mao's little red book no longer is seen as the fountain of all truth.

For the Soviet system to survive in the 1920s, it needed legitimization. Thus, an important reason for Stalin's success in seizing and maintaining power was his cannonization of Lenin, wrapping himself in Lenin's mantle, and turning the two-score plus volumes of Lenin's utterances and writings into what became Soviet constitutional law. As a result the Politburo monopolizes not only Soviet political decision making, but also what passes for Soviet constitutional review, a function which, in the United States, is the ultimate prerogative of the supreme court, or in the United Kingdom, the whole parliament. The Politburo has enormous judicial power. Yet, as prolific as Lenin was, as pragmatic as he claimed to be, not all possible changes can be justified easily by his words.

Stalin was successful in deifying Lenin. Prominent posters proclaim "Lenin Lives!" Lenin is Always with Us!" The price has been an imposition of limitations upon the leadership's options for innovation, stemming in part from the limited vision of those acceptable in the ranks of the Politburo. Not since the exile of Trotsky has there been any public debate among the standing members of the Politburo over the essentials of the Marxist-Leninist corpus.

China is undergoing a reformation; the USSR has had none. What reformation there has been in the interpretation of the sacred doctrine has been outside the boundaries of the inner empire, resulting in the most serious of all charges, blasphemy of the sacred Lenin writ, charges that have been leveled from time to time at such heretics as Tito and, especially, Mao. Not so ideologically frozen, the PRC leadership has changed its mind about the role of a United States in world affairs. Internally, the Chinese have inaugurated profound changes, including the abandonment of the rural communes. In the past, and for any foreseeable future, such changes are unthinkable in the USSR.

Gorbachev's past words and deeds suggest that he just may attempt to impose major economic and administrative changes, especially in the rural USSR. However, can he go so far as to claim that the Leninist prescribed collectivized system is fundamentally flawed? Constrained by the holy writ (which is not so holy in a PRC, Hungary or Yugoslavia) any innovation must be squared with the unchallengeable dicta of Lenin.

THIRD: THE POLITBURO IS TRAPPED BY PAST SOVIET SUCCESSES. They too believe that, "If it isn't broke, don't fix it." The system survived the enormous upheavals of the 1920s and 1930s. The system survived the awful Hitler challenge. Moreover, the leaders repeatedly argue that the USSR did it all by itself. (10) The help from the allies was insignificant. Most important of all, they are immensely proud of the fact that under the Leninist-Stalinist leadership system, the USSR was transformed from a backward, third-rate nation to one of the world's two superpowers. True, Andropov, Chernenko and, especially, Gorbachev have admitted to some, even important, imperfections, but not in the system that they believe responsible for Soviet success. The system is not broken; it cannot fail. All that needs to be done is some fine tuning of the Soviet machine as it progresses along the same familiar path.

FOURTH: THE POLITBURO IS CONSTRAINED BY THE RULING HIERARCHY OF ITS OWN MAKING. The members are limited by the bureaucracy from which they come and upon which they are dependent for their continued existence in office.

The men in the Kremlin are not fools. Yet like all human beings, they are creatures of the environment in which they operate. However, unlike the surroundings that are imposed on most mortals, much of the Politburo's environment is of the members' own making. They and their predecessors have made the Soviet rules of the game. As in the case of the British parliament, the Politburo has the legal authority to declare a man a woman.

A word from Stalin could cost the life of a Soviet citizen. A speech by Khrushchev could initiate the abandonment of the MTS. Gorbachev and his colleagues, should they so decide, can decree a change in the flow of major Soviet rivers from North to South. But, can they decree a change in the behavior of the prefects upon which much of their power rests? How easily can they change the attitudes and behavior of a people who for 1,000 years have known only authoritarian rule?

After Stalin, Khrushchev and his successors chose to replace the stick of mass police terror with the carrot of improved living standards. However, not only did they neglect the bureaucracy and the prefects who were trained under the system of terror but they, especially Brezhnev, encouraged the further intrenchment of the provincial Party secretaries. Here, then, is the central dilemma of the 1980s. Deprived of the use of terror to force the population into line, the prefects, who primarily are responsible for getting things done, overwhelmingly resist promoting worker incentives in ways which, inevitably, would weaken both the prefects' authority and their remaining power. This, of course, was what Gorbachev meant when he said: "[N]ot all of our cadres have given up inertia, old patterns... Not all have turned out to be psychologically prepared for work under new conditions,..." (11)

Brezhnev's program was to freeze the status quo. His immediate successors, had they wanted to make major changes, did not live long enough to move the Soviet Leviathan. Pointing to Gorbachev's relative youth and the stagnation of the Soviet system in recent decades, legions of Western observers have, in effect, pronounced that a new generation has come to power in the USSR and that profound change must be in the offing. Perhaps, but the past record, plus the rules of the Soviet leadership game, will not support such a view. As documented above, Gorbachev is not a newcomer, an outsider, and emphatically not the leader of some sort of Soviet political opposition that has been voted into power with a mandate to impose major reforms. Gorbachev is a product of the Soviet system. More than any member of the British parliament is a creature of that body, more than any US senator is the epitomy of that exclusive club, Gorbachev is a product of the Soviet Politburo system.

Obviously, the colleagues in the Politburo club who chose Gorbachev as their First Secretary decided that putting another old man in the post, destined to die in a few years' time, was no longer desirable. Surely, similar considerations must have been operating when a relatively young Khrushchev and a relatively young Brezhnev were given the top position. Also, as I have speculated, the fact that Gorbachev has special agricultural credentials probably is not just coincidental. Quite possibly Gorbachev has a mandate from his colleagues to move against the food problem, the most serious of all the problems of a faltering economy, but does that mandate leave him free to do whatever he feels necessary, regardless of the consequences? Numerous Western students of the Soviet system have concluded, as has this analyst, that meaningful agricultural reform cannot be confined within the boundaries of the farms. The entire economic system needs to be overhauled to create some sort of genuine marketplace mechanism, if worker incentive and initiative are to be unleashed. Ultimately, initiative and response to incentive are self-willed.

Unless they are Don Quixotes, human beings exercise initiative only when they feel they have a realistic chance of accomplishing what they set out to do. Incentives meant to increase productivity or efficiency must be accompanied by the means necessary to achieve such ends. Increased labor productivity is a major Soviet goal and, as in all industrial societies, the reliability of manufacturers and suppliers is crucial to achieving the goal. In market economies reliable manufacturers and suppliers are encouraged by satisfied customers. Local producers --e.g., farms and small industries-- turn to other sources for their inputs, such as tools and spare parts, if current manufacturers and suppliers prove to be unreliable. That option is not open to Soviet customers. Indeed, they are not customers in the sense of having any meaningful control over what they purchase from whom. Soviet industry produces what the planners tell them to produce. Soviet industrial managers are rewarded and punished by higher Party and state officials. They are largely insulated from user satisfaction. Given such relationships, Soviet industrialists don't give a damn about the ultimate users. Soviet users know this. They experience the results of such relationships by being faced with unwanted or substandard machines and materials and a chronic shortage of spare parts. As a result, a major block to worker initiative and incentive is that more often than not the workers and farmers are denied the means of production necessary to increase efficiency and output.

Gorbachev knows the problem. He has said as much many times, but neither he nor any of his Politburo colleagues have ever said that adopting a market-place economy is the price that must be paid for successful economic reform. Such a reform would cost dearly in terms of central, emphatically Politburo, economic and political controls over the Soviet Union and its people.

Not only would the wholesale changes speculated about here cost the Politburo important aspects of its power, but they would threaten many of the powers of the regional and local apparatchiky upon which the system largely rests. Not surprisingly, therefore, when Gorbachev and his supporters discussed some of the problems encountered in introducing the collective contract system, key among the points raised was resistance from those below, who are responsible for implementing the scheme. For example, two Soviet authors noted that they had observed "a reluctance upon the part of managers to relinquish much of the power they now hold...." (12)

The Soviet Politburo probably holds the single most awesome collection of powers of any body of human beings in the world but, like Gulliver, it can be rendered virtually powerless by the Lilliputians of an unresponsive bureaucracy.

Speculating on the ultimate fate of the ZVENO in 1960, Leonard Schapiro wrote that what finally would emerge in the countryside would be what the leadership judges to be best "from the point of view of party control..." (13) In the words of Hamlet: "Ay, there's the rub!"

Having not foreseen Gobrachev's rise to the top, and agreeing with the maxim spelled out by Schapiro in 1960, this writer concluded in 1984 that the collective contract scheme probably would go the way of the Liberman proposals and find itself in the ashbin of Soviet history. (14)

Now, given the events of 1985, especially Gorbachev's selection as the First Secretry of the CPSU, the possibility that major change will be attempted, once Gorbachev has a clear Politburo majority, cannot wholly be ruled out, but still it is far from certain. Can Gorbachev succeed where Khrushchev failed?

Beyond the actuality of introducing fundamental domestic economic reform, there is one other major move the Politburo can make which, if taken, would greatly ease the strain on the economy. Moreover, the move would be a major harbinger of a Kremlin resolve to set the Soviet economic house in order.

Even less than most nations, including the US, the Soviet Union cannot afford both guns and butter. The Soviet leaders fear the possibility of nuclear war and this is a major reason they returned to the disarmament negotiations. However, beyond the genuine fear of major war, there is the unspoken Kremlin recognition that an escalation of the arms race would be devastating to Soviet hopes to improve the domestic economy, especially to satisfy Soviet consumer demand. Therefore, a major indicator that the Politburo is determined to improve the domestic economy would be their willingness to make the compromises necessary to reduce genuinely the enormous burden of Soviet defense expenditures. (15)

Again, however, a shift of investment from armaments to industry and agriculture would not be enough in itself to solve the Soviet economic problem. Gorbachev knows that labor productivity on Soviet farms and in Soviet factories is far behind that of other major industrialized nations. That is the central problem demanding solution. Although I have supplied the italics, I will let Gorbachev have the last word:

> [T]o bring about a RADICAL TURN... [toward greater efficiency] we must not relax our efforts. On the contrary, we must step them up. It is a matter of primary importance to refine planning and management, and methods of running the economy, improve organization, strengthen discipline, enhance responsibility in all sections and to ENCOURAGE IN EVERY WAY CREATIVE INITIATIVE BY THE MASSES. (16)

NOTES

1. Stefan Headlund, CRISIS IN SOVIET AGRICULTURE, New York: St. Martin's Press, 1984, pp. 211 & 212.

2. Seweryn Bialer, STALIN'S SUCCESSORS: LEADERSHIP STABILITY AND CHANGE IN THE SOVIET UNION, New York: Cambridge University Press, 1980, p. 303.

3. Although there have been many time in history when the regimes that have ruled Tsarist Russia and the Soviet Union have been in serious trouble, one of the worst periods came in the early part of the seventeenth century. A false Dmitri (pretender to the throne) challenged the leadership, and received much support from the peasants, the Cossacks and the Poles. As a result of the confusion and chaos which persisted for many years, the period came to be known as "The Time of Troubles." The old regime fell and the new Romanov dynasty was elevated to the throne.

4. Gorbachev's "Report," PRAVDA, October 16, 1985. Here, and elsewhere, when translations of such documents are available in such sources as MOSCOW NEWS, those translations have been used.

5. Ibid.

6. PRAVDA, October 26, 1985.

7. Gorbachev's "Report," Op. Cit.

8. George W. Simmonds, (Ed.), SOVIET LEADERS, New York: Thomas Y. Crowell Company, 1967, p. 1.

9. A. A. Gromyko and B. N. Ponomarev, (Eds.). SOVIET FOREIGN POLICY 1917-1980, Moscow: Progress Publishers, 1980.

10. Reading the official history of Soviet foreign policy leaves a strong impression that the USSR's allies in World War II probably caused the Soviet Union as much harm as they did good. See Gromyko and Ponamarov, Op. Cit.

11. Gorbachev's "Report," Op. Cit.

12. G. Martyshkin and Yu. Proskurin, "For a Broad Introduction of the Collective Contract System," EKONOMIKY SEL'SKOGO KHOZYAISTVA, No. 5, April, 1983, pp. 72-77.

13. Leonard Schapiro THE COMMUNIST PARTY OF THE SOVIET UNION, New York: Random House, 1960, p. 515.

14. Roy D. Laird and Betty A. Laird, "The Zveno and Collective Contracts: The End of Soviet Collectivization?" in a forthcoming volume from The Seventh Interntional Conference on Soviet and Eastern European Agriculture, Paris-Grignon, July 9-12, 1984.

15. There are, of course, two sides to the disarmament deadlock. The US, too, must make concessions. However, at this point in time, I am persuaded that the Soviet leaders

have not done all they might to further an agreement. For example, I believe their willingness to give on the matter of on-the-site verification would go a long way toward breaking the deadlock.

16. Gorbachev's "Report," Op. Cit.

Appendix: Chronology of Politburo Members

POLITBURO INCUMBENCIES BY DATE OF FIRST (AND SECOND) ENTRY
(As of October, 1985)

a Family Back.	b Nation- ality	Year into Party	c Higher Ed.	d Military Exp.	e Repub. or Region 1st Sec	f Years Cand. Politburo or Presidium	f Years Full Politburo or Presidium
FULL VOTING MEMBERS							
BUBNOV, Andrey Sergeyevich, 1883-1940							
Wkr?	Russ	1905	Ag	Cmdr	----	----	1917-1919?
KAMENEV, Lev Borisovich, 1883-1936							
Int	Jewish	1901	Univ	----	----	1926-1927	1917-1926
LENIN, Vladimir Il'ich, 1870-1924							
Int	Russ	1898	Lw	----	----	----	1917-1924
SOKOL'NIKOV, Grigoriy Yakovlevich, 1888-1939							
Wkr?	Russ	1905	Lw Ecn	Cmdr	----	1924-1925	1917-1919?
STALIN, Iosif Vissarionovich, 1879-1953							
Wkr	Georg	1898	Theo	Fst	----	----	1917-1953
TROTSKY, Lev Davidovich, 1879-1940							
Int	Jewish	1902?	Coll	CmsMA	----	----	1917-1926
ZINOV'YEV, Grigoriy Yevseyevich, 1883-1936							
Wkr?	Russ	1903	Univ	----	Gorod	----	1917-1920 1924-1926
KRESTINSKIY, Nikolay Nikolayevich, 1888-1938							
Wkr?	Russ	1907?	Lw	----	Oblast	----	1919-1920
BUKHARIN, Nikolay Ivanovich, 1888-1938							
Int	Russ	1906	Ecn	----	----	1919-1920	1920-1929
PREOBRAZHENSKIY, Yevgeniy Alekseyevich, 1886-1937							
Int	Russ	1904?	----	----	----	----	1920-1921?
SEREBRYAKOV, Leonid Petrovich, 1890-1937							
Wkr	Russ	1912?	----	Cmdr	----	----	1920-1921?
TOMSKY, Mikhail Pavlovich, 1880-1936							
Wkr	Russ?	1904	----	----	----	----	1922-1929
RYKOV, Aleksey Ivanovich, 1881-1938							
Wkr?	Russ	1902	Lw	Cmdr	----	----	1924-1930

Sect. or Org. [g]	Presidium Sup. Sov. [g]	Concil of Ministers [g]	Other Important Experience	Travel Outside Bloc	Why Off Politb.	Cause of Death [h]
Yes	----	----	Purg	----	Expl	Ntrl?
----	Prs	----	ImPurg	Some	Expl	Exec
Fst	----	Pm	Founded Bols	----	Died	Ntrl
----	----	Yes	Gos Impurg	----	Expl	Ntrl?
Fst	Yes	Pm	CmsNts	----	Died	Ntrl
Yes	----	Yes	CmsMA ForCms	Much	Expl	Murd
----	Yes	----	---- ImPurg	----	Rem Expl	---- Exec
Yes	----	----	ImPurg	----	Expl	Exec
----	----	----	EdPrv ImPurg	Some	Expl	Exec
Yes	----	----	Impurg	----	Expl	Ntrl?
Yes	----	Yes	ImPurg	Little	Expl	Exec
----	----	Yes	TU Purg	----	Expl	Suic
Yes	----	Pm	Impurg MVD	----	Expl	Exec

POLITBURO INCUMBENCIES BY DATE OF FIRST (AND SECOND) ENTRY (Continued)

Name	a Family Back.	b Nation- ality	Year into Party	c Higher Ed.	d Military Exp.	e Repub. or Region 1st Sec	f Years Cand. Politburo or Presidium	f Years Full Politburo or Presidium
ZINOV'YEV, Grigoriy Yevseyevich, 1883-1936	Wkr?	Russ	1903	Univ	----	Gorod	----	1924-1926
KALININ, Mikhail Ivanovich, 1975-1946	Peas	Russ	1898	----	----	----	1919-1926?	1926-1946?
MOLOTOV, Vyacheslav Mikhaylovich, 1890-	Peas	Russ	1906	Poly	----	----	1924?-1926	1926-1957
RUDZUTAK, Yan Ernestovich, 1887-1938	Peas	Lat?	1905	----	----	----	1924?-1926 1934-1937	1926-1932
VOROSHILOV, Kliment Yefremovich, 1881-1969	Peas	Russ	1903	----	Mshl	----	----	1926-1960
KUYBYSHEV, Valerian Vladimirovich, 1888-1935	Int	Russ	1904	Lw	Cmdr	----	----	1927-1935
KAGANOVICH, Lazar Moissevich, 1893-	Peas	Jewish	1911	----	Cmdr	Ukrain	1927-1930	1930-1957
KOSIOR, Stanislav Vikent'yevich, 1889-1939	Wkr	Polish	1907	----	Cmdr	Ukrain	1927-1930	1930-1939?
ORDZHONNIKDZE, Grigoriy Konstantinovich, 1886-1937	Peas	Gorg?	1907	----	Cmdr	Krai	1926-1930	1930-1937
ANDREEV, Andrei Andreevich, 1895-1971	Peas	Russ	1914	----	----	----	1927-1934	1934-1952?
KIROV, Sergey Mironovich, 1886-1934	Wkr?	Russ	1904	Eng	Cmdr	Gorord	1927-1934	1934-1934
CHUBAR, Vlas Yakovlevich, 1891-1939	Peas	Ukrain?	1904?	Poly	Cmdr	Ukrain	1927-1935	1935-1937?
MIKOYAN, Ansastas Ivonovich, 1895-1978	Peas	Arm	1915	Theo	----	Krai	1926-1935	1935-1937?
KHRUSHCHEV, Nikita Sergeevich, 1894-1971	Peas	Russ	1918	Poly	LtG	Oblast	1935-1939	1939-1964

g Sect. or Org.	g Pre- sidium Sup. Sov.	g Council of Ministers	Other Important Experience	Travel Outside Bloc	Why Off Politb.	h Cause of Death
----	----	----	ImPurg	----	Expl	Exec
----	Prs	----	----	----	Hlth	Ntrl
Yes	Yes	Pm	ForMin	Much	Expl	----
----	Yes	Yes	ImPurg	Some	Expl	Ntrl?
Yes	Prs	Yes	----	Some	Hlth	Ntrl
Yes	----	Yes	Gos	----	Died	Ntrl
Yes	----	Yes	APG	----	Expl	----
Yes	Yes	----	ImPurg	----	Expl	Ntrl?
Yes	----	Yes	----	----	Died	Suic
Yes	Yes	Yes	Ag TU	----	Rem	Ntrl
Yes	Yes	----	----	----	Died	Murd
----	----	----	ImPurg	----	Expl	Ntrl?
----	Prs	Yes	----	Much	Hlth	Ntrl
Fst	----	Pm	----	Much	Hlth	Ntrl

POLITBURO INCUMBENCIES BY DATE OF FIRST (AND SECOND) ENTRY (Continued)

a Family Back.	b Nation- ality	Year into Party	c Higher Ed.	d Military Exp.	e Repub. or Region 1st Sec	f Years Cand. Politburo or Presidium	f Years Full Politburo or Presidium
ZHDANOV, Andrey Aleksandrovich, 1896-1948							
fInt	Russ	1912?	----	Cmdr	Oblast	1935-1939	1939-1948
BERIYA, Lavrentii Pavlovich, 1893-1953							
Peas	Georg	1917	Poly	Mshl	Georg	1939-1946	1946-1953
MALENKOV, Georgii Maksimilianovich, 1902-							
Wkr?	Russ	1920	----	Cmdr	----	1941-1946	1946-1957
VOZNESENSKIY, Nikolay Alekseyevich, 1903-1950							
Int	Russ	B1924	PolyA	----	----	1941-1947	1947-1949
BULGANIN, Nikolai Aleksandrovich, 1895-1975							
Wkr?	Russ	1917	----	Mshl	----	1946-1948	1948-1958
KOSYGIN, Aleksey Nikolaevich, 1904-1980							
Wkr?	Russ	1927	Poly	----	----	1946-1948 1957-1960	1948-1952 1960-1980
ANDRIANOV, Vasilii Mikhailovich, 1902-							
Wkr?	Russ	Nd	Nd	Nd	Gorod	----	1952-1953
ARISTOV, Averkii Borisovich, 1903-1973							
Wkr?	Russ	1921	Poly	----	Oblast	----	1952-1953 1957-1961
CHESNOKOV, Dmitrii Ivanovich, 1910-1973							
Wkr?	Russ	Nd	Univ?	Nd	Krai	----	1952-1953
IGNAT'YEV, Semen Denisovich, 1904-							
Wkr?	Tatar?	Nd	Nd	Nd	Oblast	----	1952-1953
KOROTCHENKO, Dem'yan Sergeevich, 1894-1969							
Peas	Ukrain	1918	PolA	Cmdr	----	1957-1961	1952-1953
KUUSINEN, Otto Vil'gel'movich, 1881-1964							
Wkr?	Fin	1904	Univ	Cmdr	----	----	1952-1953 1957-1964
KUZNETSOV, Vasilii Vasil'evich, 1901-							
Peas	Russ	1927	Eng	----	----	1944-1952 1977-1985	1952-1953
MALYSHEV, Vyacheslav Aleksandrovich, 1902-1957							
Int	Russ	1926	Poly	ClG	----	----	1952-1953

Sect. or Org.[g]	Presidium Sup. Sov.[g]	Council of Ministers[g]	Other Important Experience	Travel Outside Bloc	Why Off Politb.	Cause of Death[h]
Yes	----	Yes	----	----	Died	Ntrl
----	----	Yes	MVD Mshl	----	Expl	Exec
Fst	----	Pm	APG	Some	Expl	----
----	----	Yes	Gos	----	Expl	Exec
----	----	Pm	APG	Much	Expl	Ntrl
----	----	Yes Pm	Gos	Much Much	Rem Hlth	---- Ntrl
----	----	----	FstLen	----	Rem	----
---- Yes	----	----	Koms TU Amb	---- Some	Rem Rem	---- Ntrl
----	----	----	EdKom Prof	----	Rem	Ntrl
Yes	Yes	----	MVD	----	Hlth	----
----	Yes	----	----	----	Rem	Ntrl
---- Yes	Yes	----	Prs KarFin	Some Some	Rem Died	---- Ntrl
Yes	Yes	----	Amb Dip TU	Much	Rem	----
----	----	Yes	----	----	Rem	Ntrl

POLITBURO INCUMBENCIES BY DATE OF FIRST (AND SECOND) ENTRY (Continued)

a Family Back.	b Nation-ality	Year into Party	c Higher Ed.	d Military Exp.	e Repub. or Region 1st Sec	f Years Cand.	f Years Full
						Politburo or Presidium	
MEL'NIKOV, Leonid Georgievich, 1906-1981							
Wkr?	Russ	1928	Poly	----	Ukrain	1953-1956	1952-1953
MIKHAILOV, Nikolai Aleksandrovich, 1906-1982							
Wkr?	Russ	1930	Univ?	----	----	----	1952-1953
PERVUKHIN, Mikhail Georgievich, 1904-1978							
Wkr?	Russ	1919	Eng	LtG	----	1957-1961	1952-1957
PONOMARENKO, Panteleimon Kondrat'evich, 1902-							
Wkr?	Russ	1925	Eng	Cmdr	Kazak	1953-1956	1952-1953
SABUROV, Maksim Zakharovich, 1900-							
Wkr?	Russ	1920	Inst	Cmdr	----	----	1952-1957
SHKIRYATOV, Matevi Mikhailovich, 1883-1954							
Wkr?	Russ	1906	----	Cmdr	----	----	1952-1953
SHVERNIK, Nikolai Mikhailovich, 1888-1970							
Wkr?	Russ	1905	----	Cmdr	Oblast	1939-1952 1953-1957	1952-1953 1957-1964
SUSLOV, Mikhail Andreevich, 1902-1982							
Peas	Russ	1921	Ecn	Cmdr	Oblast	----	1952-1953 1955-1982
KIRICHENKO, Aleksey Illarionovich, 1908-1975							
Peas	Ukrain	1930	Eng	----	Ukrain	1953-1955	1955-1960
SUSLOV, Mikhail Andreevich (Reentry), 1902-1982							
Peas	Russ	1921	Ecn	Cmdr	Oblast	----	1955-1982
ARISTOV, Averkii Borisovich, 1903-1973							
Wkr?	Russ	1921	Poly	----	Oblast	----	1957-1961
BELYAEV, Nikolai Il'ich, 1903-1966							
Peas	Russ?	1921	Ecn	----	Krai	----	1957-1960
BREZHNEV, Leonid Il'ich, 1906-1982							
Wkr?	Russ	1931	Eng	LtG	Kazak	1952-1953 1956-1957	1957-1982
FURTSEVA, Ekaterina Alekseevna, 1910-1974							
Wkr	Russ	1930	Poly	----	Gorod	1956-1957	1957-1961

Sect. or Org.[g]	Presidium Sup. Sov.[g]	Council of Ministers[g]	Other Important Experience	Travel Outside Bloc	Why Off Politb.	Cause of Death[h]
----	----	Yes	----	----	Rem	Ntrl
Yes	----	----	AgP Koms Amb	Some	Rem	Ntrl
----	----	Yes	Amb Koms	Some	Rem	Ntrl
Yes	----	Yes	Amb Dip	Much	Rem	----
----	----	Yes	Gos Koms	Much	Rem	----
----	----	----	----	----	Rem	Ntrl
----	Prs	----	TU	Some	Rem	----
			TU	Some	Rem	Ntrl
Yes	Yes	----	AgP	----	Rem	----
Yes				Much	Died	Ntrl
Yes	----	----	----	----	Rem	Ntrl
Yes	----	----	AgP	Much	Died	Ntrl
Yes	----	----	Amb Koms Tu	Some	Rem	Ntrl
Yes	Yes	----	----	----	Rem	Ntrl
Fst	Prs	Yes	----	Much	Died	Ntrl
Yes	----	Yes	CltMin	Much	Rem	Ntrl

POLITBURO INCUMBENCIES BY DATE OF FIRST (AND SECOND) ENTRY (Continued)

a Family Back.	b Nation- ality	Year into Party	c Higher Ed.	d Military Exp.	e Repub. or Region 1st Sec	f Years Cand.	f Years Full
						Politburo or Presidium	
IGNATOV, Nikolai Alekseevna, 1901-1966							
Peas	Russ	1924	PolA	----	Oblast	1952-1953	1957-1961
KOZLOV, Frol Romanovich, 1908-1965							
Peas	Russ	1926	Poly	----	Oblast	1957-1957	1957-1964
KUUSINEN, Otto Vil'gel'movich (Reentry), 1881-1964							
Wkr?	Fin	1904	Univ	Cmdr	----	----	1957-1964
MUKHITDINOV, Nuritdin Akramovich, 1917-							
Wkr	Uzb?	1942	Some	Cmdr	Uzb	1956-1957	1957-1961
SHVERNIK, Nikolai Mikhailovich (Reentry), 1888-1970							
Wkr?	Russ	1905	----	Cmdr	Oblast	1953-1957	1957-1965
ZHUKOV, Georgii Konstantinovich, 1896-1974							
Peas	Russ	1919	MilA	Mshl	----	1956-1957	1957-1957
KOSYGIN, Aleksey Nikolaevich (Reentry), 1904-1980							
Wkr?	Russ	1927	Poly	----	----	1957-1960	1960-1980
PODGORNY, Nikolai Viktorovich, 1903-							
Wkr?	Ukrain	1930	Poly	----	Ukrain	1958-1960	1960-1977
POLYANSKY, Dmitrii Stepanivich, 1917-							
Peas	Ukrain	1939	Poly	----	Oblast	1958-1960	1960-1976
VORONOV, Gennadii Ivanovich, 1910-							
Peas	Russ	1931	PolA	----	Oblast	1961-1961	1961-1973
KIRILENKO, Andrei Pavlovich, 1906-							
Peas	Russ	1931	Poly	Cmdr	Oblast	1957-1961	1962-1982
SHELEPIN, Aleksandr Nikolaevich, 1918-							
Wkr?	Russ	1940	Inst	Cmdr	----	----	1964-1975
SHELEST, Petr Efimovich, 1908-							
Wkr?	Ukrain	1928	Poly	----	Oblast	1963-1964	1964-1973
MAZUROV, Kirill Trofimovich, 1914-							
Peas	Bel	1940	Poly	Cmdr	Bel	1957-1965	1965-1978

g Sect. or Org.	g Pre- sidium Sup. Sov.	g Council of Ministers	Other Important Experience	Travel Outside Bloc	Why Off Politb.	h Cause of Death
Yes	----	Yes	----	----	Rem	Ntrl
Yes	Yes	Yes	----	----	Hlth	Ntrl
Yes	----	----	Prs KarFin	Some	Died	Ntrl
Yes	----	----	Dip	Some	Rem	----
----	----	----	TU	Some	Rem	Ntrl
----	----	Yes	DfMin	Much	Expl	Ntrl
----	----	Pm	----	Much	Hlth	Ntrl
Yes	Prs	----	----	Some	Rem	Ntrl
----	----	Yes	Ag Amb	Some	Rem	----
Yes	----	Yes	Ag	Some	Rem	Ntrl
Yes	----	----	----	Little	Rem?	Ntrl
Yes	----	Yes	KGB Koms	----	Hlth	----
----	----	----	Dip	Some	Rem	----
----	----	----	----	Some	Hlth	----

POLITBURO INCUMBENCIES BY DATE OF FIRST (AND SECOND) ENTRY (Continued)

a Family Back.	b Nation- ality	Year into Party	c Higher Ed.	d Military Exp.	e Repub. or Region 1st Sec	f Years Cand.	f Years Full
						Politburo or Presidium	
PEL'SHE, Arvid Yanovich, 1899-1984							
Wkr?	Lat	1915	PolA	Cmdr	Lat	----	1966-1982
GRISHIN, Viktor Vasil'evich, 1914-							
Wkr	Russ	1939	Poly	----	Gorod	1961-1971	1971-
KULAKOV, Fedor Davydovich, 1918-1978							
Wkr?	Russ	1940	Ag	----	Krai	----	1971-1978
KUNAEV, Dinmukhamed Akhmedovich, 1912-							
Int	Kazak	1939	Poly	----	Kazak	1966-1971	1971-
SHCHERBITSKY, Vladimir Vasil'evich, 1918-							
Wkr	Ukrain	1941	Poly	Cmdr	Ukrain	1961-1963 1965-1971	1971-
ANDROPOV, Yurii Vladimirovich, 1914-1984							
Wkr?	Russ	1939	Univ	Gen	----	1966-1973	1973-1984
GRECHKO, Andrei Antonovich, 1903-1976							
Peas	Ukrain	1928	MilA	Mshl	----	----	1973-1976
GROMYKO, Andrei Andreevich, 1909-							
Peas	Russ	1931	Ecn	----	----	----	1973-
ROMANOV, Grigorii Vasil'evich, 1923-							
Peas	Russ	1944	Poly	----	Oblast	1973-1976	1976-1985
USTINOV, Dmitrii Fedorovich, 1908-1984							
Wkr	Russ	1927	Eng	Mshl	----	1965-1976	1976-1984
CHERNENKO, Konstantin Ustinovich, 1911-1985							
Peas	Russ	1931	Ped	Cmdr	Oblast	1977-1978	1978-1985
TIKHONOV, Nikolai Aleksandrovich, 1905-							
Int	Ukrain	1940	Eng	----	----	1978-1979	1979-
GORBACHEV, Mikhail Sergeevich, 1931-							
Peas	Russ	1952	Lw	----	Krai	1979-1980	1980-
ALIEV, Geidar Alievich, 1923-							
Wkr	Azeri	1945	Hist	MjG	----	1976-1982	1982-

g Sect. or Org.	g Pre- sidium Sup. Sov.	g Council of Ministers	Other Important Experience	Travel Outside Bloc	Why Off Politb.	h Cause of Death
----	----	----	Dip Teach	Some	Rem	Ntrl
----	Yes	----	----	Much	----	----
Yes	----	Yes	Ag	----	Died	Ntrl
----	Yes	----	----	Some	----	----
----	----	Yes	----	Little	----	----
Fst	Prs	Yes	KGB	Some	Died	Ntrl
----	----	Yes	DfMin	Some	Died	Ntrl
----	Prs	Yes	Ag Amb Dip ForMin Prof	Much	----	----
Yes	Yes	----	FstLen	Much	Rem	----
Yes	----	Yes	DfMin	Some	Died	Ntrl
Fst	Prs	----	----	Much	Died	Ntrl
----	----	Pm	Gos	Much	----	----
Fst	----	----	Ag Koms	Much	----	----
----	----	Yes	NKVD, KGB, MVD	Some	----	----

POLITBURO INCUMBENCIES BY DATE OF FIRST (AND SECOND) ENTRY (Continued)

a Family Back.	b Nation-ality	Year into Party	c Higher Ed.	d Military Exp.	e Repub. or Region 1st Sec	f Years Cand.	f Years Full
						Politburo or Presidium	
SOLOMENTSEV, Mikhail Sergeevich, 1913-							
Peas	Russ	1940	Poly	----	Oblast	1971-1983	1983-
VOROTNIKOV, Vitalii Ivanovich, 1926-							
Wkr?	Russ	1947	Poly	----	Krai	1983-1983	1983-
CHEBRIKOV, Viktor Mikhailovich, 1923-							
Wkr?	Russ	1944	Eng	Cmdr	Gorod	1983-1985	1985-
LIGACHEV, Egor Kuz'mich, 1920-							
Wkr	Russ	1944	Poly	----	Obkom	----	1985-
RYZHKOV, Nikolai Ivanovich, 1929-							
Wkr	Russ?	1956	Eng	----	----	----	1985-
SHEVARDNADZE, Eduard Amvrosievich, 1928-							
Int	Georg	1948	Ped	Gen	Gorod	1978-1985	1985-
CANDIDATE ONLY MEMBERS							
DZERZHINSKIY, Feliks Edmundovich, 1877-1926							
Int	Polish?	1905?	----	Cmdr	----	1924-1926	----
FRUNZE, Mikhail Vasil'yevich, 1885-1925							
Wkr	Ukrain?	1904	Poly	CStffA	----	1924-1925	----
PETROVSKIY, Grigoriy Ivanovich, 1878-1958							
Wkr	Ukrain	1897	----	Cmdr	Ukrain	1926-1939	----
UGLANOV, Nikolay Aleksandrovich, 1886-1940							
Peas	Russ	1907	----	----	Gorod	1927-1929	----
POSTYSHEV, Pavel Petrovich, 1887-1940							
Wkr	Ukrain	1907?	----	Cmdr	Oblast	1934-1935	----
EYKHE, Robert Indrikovich, 1890-1940							
Peas	Lat	1911?	----	Cmdr	Krai	1935-1937?	----
YEZHOV, Nikolay Ivanovich, 1895-1939							
Wkr?	Russ?	1917	----	Gen	----	1937-1938?	----

Sect. or Org.[g]	Presidium Sup. Sov.[g]	Council of Ministers[g]	Other Important Experience	Travel Outside Bloc	Why Off Politb.	Cause of Death[h]
Yes	----	----	Chm CPCC	Some	----	----
----	----	----	Amb Pm RSFSR	Little	----	----
----	----	----	KGB Gen	----	----	----
Yes	----	----	POrg ForAf	Some	----	----
Yes	----	Yes	----	Little	----	----
----	----	Yes	ForMin Koms MVD FstGeorg	Some	----	----
Yes	----	----	Cheka	----	Expl	Exec?
----	----	----	CStffA	----	Died	Ntrl
----	Yes	----	----	----	Expl	Ntrl
Yes	----	Yes	ImPurg	----	Expl	Ntrl?
----	Yes	----	Impurg	----	Expl	Ntrl?
----	----	Yes	Ag Impurg	----	Expl	Ntrl?
Yes	----	Yes	Impurg MVD Gen	----	Expl	Exec?

POLITBURO INCUMBENCIES BY DATE OF FIRST (AND SECOND) ENTRY (Continued)

a Family Back.	b Nation-ality	Year into Party	c Higher Ed.	d Military Exp.	e Repub. or Region 1st Sec	f Years Cand. Politburo or Presidium	f Years Full Politburo or Presidium
SHCHERBAKOV, Aleksandr Sergeyevich, 1901-1945							
Wkr	Russ	1918	PolA	Cmdr	Oblast	1941-1945	----
PATOLICHEV, Nikolai Semenovich, 1908-							
Peas	Russ	1931	Poly	----	Bel	1952-1953	----
TEVOSYAN, Ivan Fedorovich, 1902-1958							
Wkr	Azeri	1919	Poly	Cmdr	----	1952-1953	----
VYSHINSKY, Andrei Yanuar'evich, 1883-1954							
Wkr?	Russ	1903	Lw	Cmdr	----	1952-1953	----
ZVEREV, Arsenii Grigor'evich, 1900-1969							
Peas	Russ	1919	Ecn	Cmdr	----	1952-1953	----
BAGIROV, Mir Dzhafar Abbasovich, 1896-1956							
Wkr?	Azeri	1917	Univ	Cmdr Gen	----	1953-1953	----
KABANOV, Ivan Grigor'evich, 1898-1972							
Wkr?	Russ?	Nd	Nd	Nd	Nd	1953-1958	----
PEGOV, Nikolay Mikhaylovich, 1905-							
Wkr	Russ	1930	Acad	----	Krai	1953-1956	----
YUDIN, Pavel Fedorovich, 1899-1968							
Peas	Russ	1918	Inst	Cmdr	----	1953-1959	----
SHEPILOV, Dmitrii Trofimovich, 1905-							
Wkr?	Russ?	1926	Ag Lw	MjG	----	1956-1957	----
KALNBERZIN, Yan Eduardovich, 1893-							
Wkr?	Lat	1917	Univ	Cmdr	Lat	1957-1961	----
MZHAVANDADZE, Vasilii Pavlovich, 1902-							
Wkr?	Georg	1927	MilA	LtG	Georg	1957-1972	----
POSPELOV, Petr Nikolaevich, 1898-1979							
Wkr?	Russ	1916	PolA	----	----	1957-1961	----
PUZANOV, Aleksandr Mikhailovich, 1906-							
Peas	Russ	1925	Poly	----	Oblast	1957-1962	----

g Sect. or Org.	g Pre- sidium Sup. Sov.	g Council of Ministers	Other Important Experience	Travel Outside Bloc	Why Off Politb.	h Cause of Death
----	----	Yes	Koms	----	Died	Ntrl
----	Yes	----	Dip	Much	Rem	----
----	----	Yes	Amb	Some	Rem	Ntrl
----	----	Yes	ForMin Prof	Much	Expl	Ntrl
----	----	Yes	Prof	----	Rem	Ntrl
----	Yes	----	MVD	----	Expl	Exec
----	----	Yes	Nd	Nd	Rem	Ntrl
Yes	Yes	Yes	Amb Dip	Much	Rem	----
----	----	----	Amb Hist Prof	----	Rem	Ntrl
Yes	----	Yes	Ag AGP APG	Much	Expl	----
----	----	----	----	----	Rem	----
----	----	----	Dip	Some	Hlth	----
Yes	----	----	Ag Hist Prof DrMLI EdPrv	----	Rem	Ntrl
Yes	----	----	Ag Amb Dip	Much	Rem	----

a Family Back.	b Nation- ality	Year into Party	c Higher Ed.	d Military Exp.	e Repub. or Region 1st Sec	f Years Cand. Politburo or Presidium	f Years Full
RASHIDOV, Sharaf Rashidovich, 1917-							
Wkr?	Uzb	1939	Ped	Cmdr	Uzb	1961-1984	----
EFREMOV, Leonid Nikolaevich (sometimes spelled Yefremov), 1912-							
Wkr?	Russ	Nd?	Nd	Nd	Oblast	1962-1966	----
DEMICHEV, Petr Nilovich, 1918-							
Wkr	Russ	1939	Eng	Cmdr	Gorod	1964-	----
MASHEROV, Petr Mironovich, 1918-1980							
Peas	Bel	1943	Pedag	Cmdr	Bel	1966-1980	----
PONAMAREV, Boris Nikolaevich, 1905-							
Int	Russ	1919	Univ	Cmdr	----	1972-	----
KISELEV, Tikhon Yakovlevich, 1917-							
Wkr?	Bel	1940	PolA	----	Bel	1980-1984	----
DOLGIKH, Vladimir Ivanovich, 1924-							
Int	Russ	1942	Eng	----	Krai	1982-	----
SOKOLOV, Sergi Leonidovich, 1911-							
Int	Russ	1937	MilA	Cmdr Mshl	----	1985-	----
TALYZIN, Nikolai Vladimirovich, 1929-							
Wkr	Russ	1960	Eng	----	----	1985-	----

g Sect. or Org.	g Pre- sidium Sup. Sov.	g Council of Ministers	Other Important Experience	Travel Outside Bloc	Why Off Politb.	h Cause of Death
----	----	----	Dip Teach	Much	Rem	----
----	----	----	----	----	Rem	----
Yes	Yes	----	CltMin	----	----	----
----	Yes	----	Koms Teach	Some	Died	Ntrl
Yes	----	----	Hist ForAf Teach	Much	----	----
----	Yes	----	----	Some	Rem	----
Yes	----	----	----	Some	----	----
----	----	Yes	DfMin	Much	----	----
----	----	Yes	CommMin	----	----	----

Bibliography

Arendt, Hannah. THE ORIGINS OF TOTALITARIANISM, New York: Meridian Books Inc., 1959.

Bialer, Seweryn. STALIN'S SUCCESSORS: LEADERSHIP STABILITY AND CHANGE IN THE SOVIE UNION, New york: Cambridge University Press, 1980, p. 157.

Breslauer, George W. KHRUSHCHEV AND BREZHNEV AS LEADERS, London: George Allen and Unwin, 1982.

Brown, Archie, and Kaiser, Michael (Eds.). THE SOVIET UNION SINCE THE FALL OF KHRUSHCHEV, London: The MacMillan Press Ltd., 1975.

Bunce, Valerie. DO NEW LEADERS MAKE A DIFFERENCE? Princeton, New Jersey: Princeton University Press, 1981.

Crowley, E. L., Lebed, A. I. and Schulz, H. E. (Eds.). PARTY AND GOVERNMENT OFFICIALS OF THE SOVIET UNION 1917-1967, Metuchen, New Jersey: The Scarecrow Press, Inc., 1969.

Crowley, Edward L., Lebed, Andrew I. and Schulz, Dr. Heinrich (Eds.), PROMINENT PERSONALITIES IN THE USSR, Metuchen, New Jersey: The Scarecrow Press, Inc., 1968.

Gromyko, A. A. and Ponomarev, B. N. (Eds.). SOVIET FOREIGN POLICY 1917-1980, Moscow: Progress Publishers, 1980.

Hedlund, Stefan. CRISIS IN SOVIET AGRICULTURE, New York: St. Martin's Press, 1984.

Kelley, Donald R. SOVIET POLITICS IN THE BREZHNEV ERA, New York: Praeger, 1980.

KHRUSHCHEV REMEMBERS (Trans. and Ed. by Strobe Talbott, Int. and Commentary by Edward Crankshaw), Boston: Little, Brown and Company 1970.

Kort, Michael. THE SOVIET COLOSSUS: A HISTORY OF THE USSR, New York: Charles Scribner's Sons, 1985.

Kraus, Herwig. THE COMPOSITION OF LEADING ORGANS OF THE CPSU (1952-1982), Munich: Supplement to the Radio Liberty Research Bulletin, 1982.

Laird, Roy D. THE SOVIET PARADIGM: AN EXPERIMENT IN CREATING A MONOHIERARCHICAL POLICY, New York: The Free Press, 1970.

Laird, Roy D., Sharp, Darwin E. and Sturtevant, Ruth. THE RISE AND FALL OF THE MTS AS AN INSTRUMENT OF SOVIET RULE, Lawrence, Kansas: The University of Kansas Publication Governmental Research Series No. 22, 1960.

Lebed, Andrew I., Schulz, Dr. Heinrich E., Taylor, Dr. Stephen S. (Eds.), WHO'S WHO IN THE USSR 1956-66, New York: The Scarecrow Press, Inc., 1966.

Lowenhardt, John. THE SOVIET POLITBURO, Edinburgh: Canongate Publishing Limited, 1982.

Medvedev, Roy A. and Medvedev, Zhores A. KHRUSHCHEV THE YEARS IN POWER, (Trans. by Andrew R. Durkin), New York: W. W. Norton and Company, 1978.

Nove, Alec. STALINISM AND AFTER, London: George Allen & Unwin Ltd, 1975.

Parrott, Bruce. POLITICS AND TECHNOLOGY IN THE SOVIET UNION, Cambridge, Massachusetts: The MIT Press, 1983.

Rahr, Alexander G. A BIOGRAPHIC DIRECTORY OF 100 LEADING SOVIET OFFICIALS, Munich: Radio Liberty, RFE/RL, August, 1984.

Riesman, David, Glazier, Nathan, and Denney, Raul, THE LONELY CROWD, Garden City: Doubleday Anchor Books, 1953.

Schapiro, Leonard. THE COMMUNIST PARTY OF THE SOVIET UNION, New York: Random House, 1960.

Schulz, Dr. Heinrich E. and Taylor, Dr. Stephen S. (Eds.), WHO'S WHO IN THE USSR 1961-62, Montreal: Intercontinental Book and Publishing Co., Ltd., 1962.

Schulz, Dr. Heinrich E., Urban, Paul K. and Lebed, Andrew I. (Eds.), WHO WAS WHO IN THE USSR, Metuchen, New Jersey: The Scarecrow Press, Inc., 1972.

Simmonds George W. (Ed.), SOVIET LEADERS, New York: Thomas Y. Crowell Company, 1967.

Ulam, Adam B. A HISTORY OF SOVIET RUSSIA, New York: Praeger, 1976

Weber, Max. ESSAYS ON SOCIOLOGY (translated and edited by Hans Gerth and C. Wright Mills), New York: Oxford University Press, 1961.

Yanov, Alexander. THE DRAMA OF THE SOVIET 1960S: A LOST REFORM, Berkeley: University of California Institute of International Studies, 1984.

Index